BARBARA FRUM

BARBARA FRUM

A Daughter's Memoir

LINDA FRUM

RANDOM HOUSE CANADA

Published in Canada by Random House of Canada, Limited, Toronto.

Canadian Cataloguing in Publication Data
Frum, Linda, 1963–
Barbara Frum: a daughter's memoir

Includes index.
ISBN 0-394-22342-X

1. Frum, Barbara, 1937-1992 2. Women journalists – Canada – Biography.
3. Women television personalities – Canada – Biography. I. Title

PN4913.F78F78 1996   070'.92   C96-930770-5

Printed and bound in the United States of America

10 9 8 7 6 5 4 3 2 1

Cover photo: Fred Phipps
Back cover photo: Biserka

For Florence and Murray,
who made her who she was.
And for Barbara and Samuel,
Miranda and Nathaniel,
so that they will know her

Acknowledgements

THE DESIRE TO WRITE this book came upon me soon after my mother's death, but I never would have pledged myself to such a project had I not been encouraged by my family. My father Murray, my brother David, my grandmother Florence, my aunt Suzy, and my uncle Gerry, each made generous editorial contributions and, even more importantly, shared their love and support during a painful and difficult period.

I owe special gratitude to David who read early drafts I was too nervous to show anyone else. Without his advice and editorial wisdom (handed out in what he calls *praise sandwiches*: "This sentence is good...these eight chapters are unintelligible...but this sentence here is *really* good!") I never would have completed this book.

Douglas Pepper, vice president and editorial director of Random House Canada is a patient and good man. His encouragement and kindness were invaluable. David Warren, a man and editor of sensitivity and insight, honoured me with his efforts. He has my admiration, affection and gratitude.

Ruth Ellen Soles, my mother's friend and former publicist for *The Journal* was the book's unofficial research assistant. I never asked a question to which she couldn't or wouldn't find an answer. She has been a great friend. I cannot thank her enough. (My other research assistant was my mother herself, who during her lifetime maintained impeccable files and clippings, which my family intends to donate soon to an educational institution.)

Many people made valuable contributions. Some are quoted in the text, others helped me formulate my ideas; still others played a vital role in my mother's life, and therefore, even if indirectly, aided in the creation of this book. My deepest thanks to: Mark Starowicz, Bob Fulford, Geraldine Sherman, Alan Wilkinson, Sally Reardon, June Callwood, Trent Frayne, Anna and Julian Porter, Susan and Tim Kotcheff, John and Isabel Bassett, Danielle Crittenden, Max Allen, Timothy Findley, Gertrude Carrel, Margaret and Amelia Faiad, Mary Lococo, Jennie Bogomolny, Grace Barnes, Willis Beese, Rivanne Sandler, Esther Simpson, Michael Kan, Howard Sutcliffe, Brigitte Shim, Nancy Erwin, Alan Borovoy, Arthur Bielfeld, Daniel Gelfant, Tamar Klunder, Ron Krant, Ken Puley, Larry Zolf, Knowlton Nash, Beth Haddon, Anne Emin, Andrea Roy, Sally Armstrong, Marie Natanson, Pam Clasper, Heather Robertson, Susan Crean, Peter Gzowski, Margaret Lyons, Charlotte Gray, George Jonas, Peter Herrndorf, Lisa Thompson, Denis Campeau, Tony Azevedo, Rosalina Cardozo, Rosemary Paulo, Sara Hirsch, Arthur Low.

My gratitude to my friends who stood by loyally as I disappeared into a haze of motherhood and writing, with extra thanks to: Carl Knutson, Anne Fenn, Ric Bienstock, Mary Webster, Alison Maclean, David Eddie, Rosemary Michel, Vicky Gall, Andrew Pepper, Devon Cross and Ellen Valero.

My father's second wife, the very kind Nancy Lockhart, gave her love and assistance in innumerable ways. My children, Barbara and Samuel, made the greatest contribution of all: they gave me joy.

Prologue

If thou didst ever hold me in thy heart,
Absent thee from felicity awhile,
And in this harsh world draw thy breath in pain,
To tell my story.

WILLIAM SHAKESPEARE, *Hamlet*

MY MOTHER NEVER asked me to tell her story. But I think she always knew that someday I would.

One morning, less than a year before my mother died, she walked down the hallway of her house to my childhood bedroom, where I had slept that night. She poked her head through the doorway and said, "I couldn't sleep last night. I was flailing about like baby Miranda [my brother's then two-month-old daughter]. I was terrified. And finally, what comforted me, what allowed me to get through the night, was the thought that, after I'm gone...I know I can count on you, Linda, to miss me."

My mother was not attempting to deprecate others in her life who adored and cherished her, although she greatly underestimated how much she would be missed and by how many. Nor was she making a subtle suggestion that I write this book — she would have snorted at the presumption of asking anyone to do anything like that.

This is a debunking age. When a great woman dies, biographers, particularly biographers who also happen to be her daughter, delight in telling us that she was not as great as we thought. They detail the most minute fractures in her feet of clay, as if these faults were the only aspect of their subject's life that mattered — or that the public might want to know.

Of course, everyone is imperfect. But around us too are exemplary lives from which we can learn. I believe that my mother's life was one of those; her faults were much less important than her strengths and virtues.

I write this book not as an expert on the CBC, or feminism, nor as an historian, but as a daughter, with all that that implies.

My mother's life has much to teach my generation of women, torn as we are between work and family. Unlike the women of the fifties, who knew (or thought they knew) that they wanted to be wives, mothers, nurturers; unlike the women of the seventies, who knew (or thought they knew) that they wanted careers and to put themselves first, my generation seems lost. We want simultaneously to be married *and* independent, mothers *and* career women, emotionally supportive *and* nobody's doormat, not even our children's.

This is not to say that we should all try to imitate Barbara Frum. My mother invented a new way of life for which she had no models. It was exhilarating, but it also meant making mistakes. She showed how much a single human life can contain.

My mother was exceptional not because she was able to reconcile the life of the working woman with the life of wife and mother — many do that. She was exceptional because she reconciled these roles brilliantly, and did more. She loved and supported her friends. She was an active citizen and a committed Jew. She was a passionate art collector, a gardener and builder of genius, and a generous yet discreet philanthropist. She infused what she touched with beauty.

"How did Barbara accomplish all that she did?" asked her brother Gerald at her memorial service. "It was as if she had mastered some mysterious alchemy that enabled her to manufacture time."

It is true that my mother stretched her day with a magician's ingenuity, but she still had to make choices and sacrifices. As a mother, she may not have given as much of her time to my brothers and myself as we might have wished. As a wife, she may have demanded that my father bend the shape of his life to hers more often than the reverse.

My mother habitually performed three tasks at once: talking on the phone, scanning files, and plucking eyebrows; cooking dinner, re-organizing the pantry, and sorting the mail. Idleness did not become her. Her days — by choice and necessity — were relentless.

On weekdays, my parents, never early risers, would wake between eight and nine to the voice of the CBC morning news. My mother would lie half awake in bed assessing the news day that awaited her. By nine, my father would emerge from the bedroom fully dressed, collect the newspapers from the front step, and sit in the dining room to await his coffee. My mother, wearing her once luxurious, now tatty, blue velour bathrobe, would head for the kettle.

She felt a Turkish respect for coffee. She ground the beans coarsely, and poured them into a plunger-style coffee-maker well past the indicator mark. She liked to sip coffee from a delicate floral demitasse cup rinsed first with hot water. And yet, despite this effort, her love and need for coffee was such that she gladly tossed back the stuff even after it had become lukewarm. I remember how often she frantically clicked her fingers at me to catch my attention. She would be on an important call, the coffee pot miserably out of reach. As I topped up her cup her face would fill with pleasure, and she would run her hand gratefully down my hair with a mother's gentleness and an addict's relief.

For reasons I never understood, my parents had a telephone system with a peculiarly shrill, upsetting ring. On weekday mornings, the ringing began no later than 9:15. The first call might be from any of a hundred people, and would be followed by a flood of other calls. With each harsh ring, my mother would roll her eyes, or sigh ironically. If the call were for my father, who received almost as many calls as she did, my mother would relax back into her chair as though given some reprieve. It never lasted long.

Despite the volume of calls, my parents refused to hire a secretary or install an answering machine. My mother had an irrational and self-destructive antipathy towards technology. And after I bought her an answering machine, extolling the ways this device could improve her life, she still sprang up to answer the telephone during meals, cursing all the way. I suspect that my mother, so used to feeling harassed, came to expect a constant level of irritation, and feared what might happen if she lost it. A journalist profiling her for a magazine once asked her what she did to relax. "I don't do anything to relax," she said. "I don't want to relax."

There was nothing relaxing about her home on a weekday morning. By 9:30 a.m. the house reverberated with jangling explosions. Perhaps Tony, my mother's cherished gardener, would be in the garden with a leaf blower, tree-trimmer, or some other machine seemingly designed to blow sound into the house. Or one of an unending series of renovations would be in progress, and the doorbells would ring incessantly. (The doorbell noise was almost as bad as the telephone's and provoked ear-splitting, high-C yelps from Diva, my mother's poodle.) The sound of stomping workboots could be heard through the halls, drills and saws would soon begin screeching. My parents' joy in open-plan architecture and sound-reflecting materials like glass and hard woods exposed the whole house to noise.

At ten o'clock, Rosalina, my parents' housekeeper of ten years, would arrive prompting loud barks of appreciation from Diva, and Rosalina would chant in return, "I love you too, Diva. I love you too." And then the postman. A non-event at most homes, at my parents' house it was a trigger for accumulated tension. After a number of unpleasant encounters with local dogs, the postman had bought himself a large German shepherd to walk with. Diva and the German shepherd enjoyed a daily bark-fest, forcing the now numerous denizens of the house to shout in order to be heard over them.

Elegant, competent, and authoritarian, Rosalina commanded great respect from my mother, who guiltily felt that the woman was under-employed, often saying that it would have been more appropriate had she managed Rideau Hall or 24 Sussex Drive. Part of the price of employing Rosalina was listening to her daily reports on the state of her marriage, her mortgage, and her health. Nodding at these monologues was another one of the many things my mother did simultaneously. Rosalina would always end her morning talk with the same question: "Mrs. Frum, what shall be for dinner tonight?"

My mother would open the pantry, stuffed with jars and cans of exotica: candied ginger, pickled radish, hearts of palm, apricot paste, baby corn, fish eggs. Frantically scanning the shelves she would despair, "Oh we have nothing! We have nothing!" Then, opening the freezer, she would take out a package of frozen chicken breasts. "I guess it'll just have to be chicken and rice again." Despite my mother's complaints that, "No one understands I'm still the one who has to worry about dinner every night," four weeknights out of five my parents ate grilled chicken and rice, invariably surprised that Rosalina had defied strict orders to use less salt in the rice and less fat in the gravy. In her Portuguese-flavoured English, Rosalina referred to gravy as "grave", and we took advantage of this to make the obvious joke. You'd think that Rosalina would just be on permanent instruction to prepare this standard meal unless otherwise instructed. But since this daily ritual of menu planning was so anti-relaxing, I have to believe that my mother enjoyed it.

Shortly before 10:30, my father would catch my mother's attention. It was time for him to leave for the office. My father is a shopping-centre developer. In his earlier career as a dentist, he had left much earlier for work. But once my mother began *The Journal*, returning home at 10:30 p.m., these morning hours were his only weekday time with her. As always, he rearranged his day to suit hers.

"Hang on, Frummy," she would call out to him on his way out the door. "Let's hear what's on *your* list."

My father would begin by holding up a pile of mail. "I'm responding to these invitations. I'm calling Bob and Geraldine about Saturday. I'm getting the painter in here for tomorrow. My secretary will renew your driver's license. I'm dropping off a cheque for Diva's hairdo bills. I'm going to talk to Howard about fixing the mailbox. And I'll pick up those bulbs you ordered from Cruickshank's."

"That's it?" my mother would ask plaintively.

"I've got a busy day, babe," my father would respond, looking sheepish.

"Don't be upset, Frummy," my mother would say with a sheepish look of her own. "I know that's a lot of things to do, but my list is even longer."

My father, who knew that this was perfectly true, never begrudged her requests for help. He once remarked about her, "There's no question who keeps our house organized, and it can be a strain on her, I admit." Of the two of them, it was my mother who described the pace of her life as "maniacal" with "chaos almost winning".

By eleven o'clock my mother's limousine driver would have arrived to take her to her hairdresser. He usually had to wait while she attended to last-minute matters around the house and got dressed. Leaving the house in the morning, my mother could look quite eccentric. After she joined *The Journal*, her body existed in two halves. The top was visible to 1.2 million viewers every day. Her bottom half, tucked beneath *The Journal* anchor desk, remained safely anonymous. Although both halves were always dressed elegantly — even on her anonymous half she wore French pumps, colourful stockings, and designer skirts — they didn't necessarily match.

From the house she went to the Yorkville salon of her hairdresser, Denis Campeau. She had decided long ago that all the CBC's in-house hairdressers "must hate my guts or they wouldn't try to make me look so awful." My mother trusted Denis, who became one of her warmest friends. But this was a problem. It was my mother's constant ambition to spend the hour it took to set her hair reading files and returning phone calls, but instead she almost always ended up talking to Denis about lawn furniture, Caribbean getaways, caterers, or peonies. Similarly she would speak with her driver, Leo, a Russian Jew, about European politics and where to buy smoked carp.

Arriving at *The Journal* at one, having picked up a sandwich in Yorkville or in the CBC cafeteria (she was believed to be the only CBC veteran who could stomach the canteen's tuna), she headed straight for her dressing room. She would collect the research folders from a plastic shelf glued to her dressing-room door, together with her mail, phone messages, and memos and prepare for the next tedious daily ritual: make-up.

As her make-up artist worked on her face, an army of story producers would march into my mother's dressing room to discuss the day's interviews, to review the previous day's, and to preview the week to come, usually throwing in a few comments about their children's progress in school or a break-up with a boyfriend. People confided in her.

Until 10:00 p.m. her life was dedicated to putting out *The Journal.* She would conduct three or four interviews a day, and in between worked in her dressing room, doing research, returning calls, and attending to personal business, including a daily call to her mother which could last as long as an hour. Gulps of fresh air came when she would take Diva out for a walk. Diva accompanied my mother to work every day except Wednesday, when Diva, whose hair had been allowed to grow until it doubled her body volume, had a grooming appointment of her own. My mother, embarrassed by this excess, explained obliquely to colleagues who noticed her weekly absence, "It's Diva's day off."

At 6:00 p.m. a production assistant brought a dinner of some sort to my mother's dressing room. My mother typically ate only enough to hold her off until she could enjoy a decent dinner at home, sharing the rest with Diva.

Some nights after the show, my father would swing by the studio to take her out to one of their preferred restaurants; otherwise, her driver would bring her back home. She would then take her chicken and rice from the oven where it would have been left to warm. She would sit at the dining table at a place-setting elegantly arranged by Rosalina earlier in the day, and pour herself a big glass of robust red wine from one of the bottles which filled my father's cellar. My father would be in the living room watching *The Journal.* At eleven o'clock, he would turn off the TV in the living room, and join my mother in the dining room. By 11:30, they would retire to their bedroom where my mother would watch *Nightline* and David Letterman, then still in its original 12:30 time slot. At 1:30, she would turn off the TV, and shoo Diva from the bedroom, as though this somehow preserved Diva from overindulgence. At day's end, she would sink into fitful sleep. By filling her day with so much, my mother was able to con all of us into the reassuring illusion that her acute lymphatic leukemia was under control, and that she was not dying.

On March 10, 1992, I made one of my regular drop-ins to my mother at work. Whenever I wanted to see her, I knew I could find her in one of two places: the studio on Mutual Street where *The Journal* was recorded, or her tiny dressing room. The CBC had given her an office which she seldom used. She was a hostage of *The Journal* and, after ten years of hosting the program, not always a happy one.

My mother used to joke that the reason she stopped going to cocktail parties after she started at *The Journal* was that she couldn't stand being asked, "How do you handle the long hours?" She hated them, and often felt bored and trapped.

I dropped in as often as three times a week. My mother was the friend to whom I confided my secrets. I knew she welcomed the distraction and the opportunity for girl-talk. For me, these visits were a chance to make up for lost time in childhood, when my mother's work too often took her away from me.

When I entered her dressing room, I always got an enthusiastic welcome. It was as if her quarantine was broken.

On that day, I came by at about three o'clock. My mother's make-up artist, Andrea, was applying thick layers of cosmetics. Lately, my mother's pale face had needed more help to look rosy. She sat in her trademark pose: make-up chair high off the ground, half-moon reading glasses held six inches from her nose so that Andrea could work on her face while my mother read the files in her lap.

I did not get my usual glad greeting. My mother was preoccupied. This troubled me because there was something I specifically wanted to tell her. I had just returned from a brief vacation in California. There, my boyfriend Tim and I had made the decision to live together. I knew my mother would not applaud. "Either you're serious or you're not. Either you're in love or you're not." I could hear her saying words before she said them. If she had taught me anything it was that life had to be lived with passion and conviction; she did not believe in half-measures.

But on that day, my mother, normally eager to discuss the trivialities of my existence on the slightest encouragement, could barely speak. After several halting attempts, the conversation stopped altogether. My mother's mood was dark and quiet. It became clear that we were waiting for Andrea to leave. In the meantime, I reached for a publisher's advance copy of Mordecai Richler's *Oh Canada! Oh Quebec!* on her make-up counter. I knew that the subject of the book, a lament for the loss of civility and tolerance in Richler's native province, was one of consuming interest to her.

"You interviewing him?" I asked.

She nodded dully. "Tomorrow."

Silence.

Since I could engage her neither on the subject of my romantic life nor on Quebec's independence, I gave up and waited. At last, my mother asked Andrea to leave the room. Now I was truly alarmed. My mother was extremely fond of Andrea, and this curt request was shockingly out-of-character.

As Andrea closed the door behind her, my mother folded her hands in her lap. She stared down at her fingers. I looked at her searchingly, fearfully.

Finally, without looking up, she said, "My blood counts won't stay up, Linny." Thick drops of tears landed in her lap. "I'm going to start needing transfusions every week. I can't keep this up."

A short while before, my mother had begun receiving bi-monthly blood transfusions. I had accompanied her to each one, and would read aloud to her as she lay on the gurney.

I tried to control my panic.

"It's okay, Mum," I said, thinking that we would find the strength to handle more transfusions. "You know I'll come with you. ..."

"You don't get it," she said, impatiently pulling an index card from her purse on which she had charted the bi-weekly results of blood tests. "Look at these numbers! And as each month goes by, my counts dip lower and lower!"

My stomach filled with dread. "Mummy..." I put my hands gently over hers. "We must keep fighting. And if we get to the point where you need my blood, or my bone marrow, or my bones, or my heart, I'll give it to you."

"I know," she said, "but it doesn't work that way."

We held each other tightly for a long time.

I was fifteen, my mother forty, in the summer of 1978, when she had first told me that she was dying. We had just been for an afternoon swim and were sitting on the wooden porch outside our kitchen, feet propped on a table, water dripping off our bodies, having an amiable chat.

As ever, I was enthralled with my mother's company. My mother, of course, was a charismatic person. But to my adolescent self, she was simply my mother, and it seemed natural and ordinary that I should desperately crave her company. Time spent with her was always precious. Summers were glorious because that was when she was on vacation from *As It Happens*.

That summer my mother had arranged that I take horseback-riding lessons at an equestrian club in North Toronto. I hated riding, but she had decided that elegant young girls should ride horses, and I had been seduced by her fantasy.

On that summer day, after a steamy morning being thrown from horses, I told her about someone I knew at school whose mother had just died from cancer. I must have recounted this story with the detached arrogance of someone uninitiated in personal tragedy. I must have been offensive, for I am certain that the confession that came out of her that day was not premeditated.

"I have cancer," she said, and then smiled. That smile gave me hope. "I get it," I thought. She was trying to teach me a lesson about not feeling superior. What a cruel way to do it!

"No you don't!" I shot back, angry at her little game.

"Yes," she continued calmly, "I do."

"This isn't funny, Mummy! You do not!" I actually thought she didn't understand the gravity of her words; that to have cancer was to die. And look at her! She was healthy and robust. Her fame as a journalist was based precisely on how aggressive she was, how strong, how fierce.

But she was relentless, and after an endless back and forth of "I do" and "You don't!" I was forced to accept the truth. She had, she told me, the same cancer that had killed her father nine years before.

The terror of that information was overwhelming. When I think back now, I cannot remember her touching or hugging me, which is odd, because she was usually so gentle and affectionate to me. Maybe on this occasion she thought it important that I comfort myself. Or maybe my memory is false for I was inconsolable. All I remember is how calm she was.

"Are you going to die!?"

"No. Not for a while."

"How do you know that?"

"Because I've already had it for five years and I'm all right."

(On that day, I fell into the family habit of referring to my mother's disease as "it" or "Mum's thing" as opposed to leukemia, which continues to be for me the most dreaded word in the English language.)

"You've had it for five years and you didn't tell me?!"

"There was no reason to tell you. I didn't think it would be good for you to think you had a sick mother. Girls your age need a strong mother. I always wanted you to feel you could be angry with me. I wanted you to have the opportunity to fight with me and not feel guilty."

"But what's going to happen now?"

"Well, at first the doctors thought I only had two years to live. Then they told me five years, and I've lived longer than that. Now they don't want to give me a number. They don't know how long I have."

"But Mummy, I need you!"

"I will be here."

"But I want you to be here when I grow up."

"I will."

"You promise?"

"I promise. I'm going to be here for a long time."

Now fourteen years later, a blink of an eye, I was in her dressing-room, filled with the same fear and inconsolable grief I had felt at age fifteen. I was amazed we had held on this long, hatefully aware that the evil we faced could not be defied forever.

By the next evening, my mother lay in a hospital bed, weak, thin, with tubes attached to her bruised arms. I had spent the day at the hospital with her. She had received a transfusion, but it seemed to have had no effect. She had asked me to bring a plastic shopping bag in which a yellow and blue cardigan she was knitting for my twenty-ninth birthday rested half-finished. She had hoped to knit through the two-hour transfusion, but she couldn't summon the strength. She never would finish the sweater.

Later that evening, my father came to the hospital to be with my mother. Soon after I got home, my telephone rang.

"Sweetheart?" she asked in a voice muffled by her struggle to hold the phone to her mouth.

"Yes, Mummy?"

"Are you suffering, sweetheart?"

The absurd generosity of her question devastated me.

"No, Mummy, I'm not suffering," I said, scarcely able to speak. Then I said more truthfully, "I'm just suffering because I don't want you to suffer and I love you so much. All I want in life is to be able to talk to you."

Her protective, maternal warmth reached me through the line, and then, with a courage I cannot fathom, she said:

"You must remember, Linda, that we've had a lot of time together. You must remember that."

Two weeks later, my mother died, at age fifty-four. It was not enough time.

March 1992, the month my mother died, was particularly frigid, even by Canadian standards. The harsh burn of the Arctic wind whipped a country already bloodied by a constitutional crisis and an economic recession. Twenty-one months before, the Meech Lake Accord had been killed off. It was already obvious that its makeshift successor, the Charlottetown Accord, would be voted down in June. The country was mired in spiritual and financial depression.

My mother took a frighteningly personal attitude toward Canada's fortunes. Even on a happy occasion in the midst of the Meech fiasco — a launch party for a book I had edited called *The Newsmakers*, a book with which she had been quite involved — my mother was unable to shake her gloom over what she feared was the impending destruction of the country. When a goofy camera crew from YTV, spoofing her and the party, approached her mockingly and offered her a swig of Scope mouthwash to better face the supposedly august company in the room, she replied spontaneously and humourlessly: "How can you joke at a time like this? I'm trying to save the country!"

"The Meech Lake debate coincided with the final phase of her illness," my brother David says in retrospect. "I think she had this sense of time running out, both for her and the country. She was like Cyrano de Bergerac, who curses his enemies one by one as he dies, and then his arch-enemy, human stupidity. Just as it was so stupid for her to die the way that she was dying — why couldn't science cope with this problem? — so it was stupid for the country to be dying in the way that it seemed to her to be dying. She died at a moment when our country was in the depths of a crisis. My theory is that that's why her death touched off such an incredible reaction."

Max Allen, a "mad genius" producer (my mother's words) who worked with her at *As It Happens*, offered me a similar theory: "When I heard Barbara had died, I thought she died because she thought the country was dying."

The morning of her death, as news of it travelled across the country, I sat grimly in my car with my boyfriend Tim, making our way from the hospital to my parents' home, where a group of their friends were meeting to plan the funeral. By 6:00 a.m. I had already picked up my mother's belongings from her hospital room and had restrained myself from the urge to strangle the smug nurse who felt the need to say: "She lived a long time for someone with leukemia, you know."

I flicked on the CBC Radio news, which led with an announcement of my mother's death.

"Do you really want to listen to that?" asked Tim.

"Yes," I murmured.

How could I explain my desire to hear about the loss of my mother, declared in such a stark way? This was the most intensely painful and private moment of my life. How surreal to have something so personal, so horrible, broadcast across the country; to hear the echo of: She's dead. She's dead. She's dead.

And yet, as I listened, I found myself grateful that such a momentous event for my family was being treated as a momentous event for Canada. I also felt anger that my mother's death was being catalogued as just one of the day's events, along with rising interest rates or record cold. I thought people would hear the announcement of her death and say casually, "Gee, that's interesting," arousing, as Tolstoy wrote, "the complacent feeling that it is he who is dead, and not I."

But this anger was dissipated soon after. Our family was told stories of people hearing the news on the radio and pulling off the road to cry, of signs appearing on people's lawns saying: "We miss you, Barbara"; of *The Journal* offices being flooded with letters. Gratitude returned.

In the weeks and months after my mother's death, my family read each of the thousands of letters; beautiful letters from friends and strangers, colleagues and distant acquaintances. I received cards from school mates I had not heard from since graduation. They were written with a gentleness and kindness that could only make you a passionate believer in the decency and goodness of people.

Most of the letters came from people who had never met my mother, but who felt her death deeply. They wrote things like, "It seems we are losing all the things that mean the most to us as Canadians." And, "... I spent much of this morning in tears. When I went to pick up my daughter at a friend's after preschool, one of the mothers noted my red eyes and asked if I was ill. I said I had been crying, and explained my reason. At once all the other women said that they too had been greatly affected by the sad news of the day, and we all feel as though we had learned of the sudden death of a friend." And, "I will miss her terribly for reasons I cannot fully understand right now, except that I know she was a wise woman who touched me intellectually and emotionally."

Mark Starowicz, my mother's producer at the CBC, collaborator and friend of twenty years, told me later: "The day she died, the faxes arrived in waves. Three hundred that morning. They were like little letters to the editor. Some were one line. Some had a few lines of poetry. Some were very effusive. It went on for a long time, but on that morning it was particularly touching because of the spontaneity. I couldn't believe it because the faxes that came in during the previous ten years came in two categories: one was we adore what you're doing, and the other was very anti-Barbara."

"How do you explain it?" I asked him.

"I can explain it," Starowicz said, "by telling you about a friend of mine who routinely criticized Barbara, but was devastated when she died. I asked him, 'Why?' And he said: 'The country senses it has lost an honest person.' She was an honest journalist. Whether you liked Barbara's handling of Thatcher or this or that, an absolute ingredient of her reputation was her incorruptibility. She might be the strict school-mistress to some, the beloved creature to another, but both sides seemed to agree that this woman was clean, this woman was incorruptible, this was an honest woman. It doesn't sound like much, but if you play it against the tableau of the decade, I think that was the answer."

Max Allen remarked: "The country had a sense of her character. Barbara was not the model of a television host; Barbara was the model of a person."

When I arrived at my parents' house, a house they had lived in together for thirty-two years, I saw my father, normally a powerful and indefatigable man, slumped on a sofa, crushed by his grief and exhaustion. In the immediate moments after her death he had moaned: "I've died too! I've died too!" and I feared the truth of what he was saying. They were as close as two people could ever dream to be. They seemed an invincible, indestructible pair; an exceptional, symbiotic couple in the eyes not only of their children, but to all who knew them.

As the informal funeral committee gathered, eyes turned to my father. What did Barbara want? A large funeral or a small one? A public memorial? Or would she have hated that?

"I don't know," said my father, startling everyone who knew him to be the keeper of my mother's mind and soul. "We never talked about this."

The rabbi asked gently: "How about a burial plot? Do you have one?"

"No," my father replied. "There's nothing. We never talked about it."

For eighteen years my mother and father had faced her terminal disease. They had not wasted a minute planning for her death.

My father delegated the decisions to a committee of my parents' closest friends. Ultimately, it was decided to hold a public memorial at Massey Hall on April 5, 1992, two weeks later. Originally, they had intended to hold the event at Convocation Hall, at the University of Toronto, my mother's Alma Mater and the place she had met my father. But it quickly became obvious that a 1200-seat auditorium would be too small. Massey Hall offered their space for free, and our family was deeply touched by that; even more to learn that IATSE, the stage workers' union, wanted to waive their fees. My father, a former chairman of the Stratford Festival and therefore well acquainted with the union, said with astonished gratitude: "They *never* do that!" CBC TV's Don Newman, who only two months earlier had lost his own son in a terrible medical accident, insisted on hosting the live coverage of the memorial on *CBC Newsworld.* A *Maclean's* magazine headline summed up what seemed to be a national outpouring of grief as "A death in the family".

During her lifetime my mother won four ACTRA awards; was an Officer of the Order of Canada; held numerous honorary degrees; helped shape two of Canada's most important journalistic institutions; and was a breakthrough female journalist and role model. She counted among her friends the most prominent members of Canadian society and although all of that was acknowledged at her memorial service, the mourners there talked about something more important.

"Who can capture the essence of Barbara Frum?" asked her brother Gerald Rosberg. "Her radiance, her courage, the resonance of her laughter, her nobility? She set high standards for everyone, but for no one higher than herself. In her own home, as in her professional life, she was the embodiment of honesty, integrity, respect for tradition, love of learning, and kindness."

I know my mother would have been pleased to be remembered for her character, not only her accomplishments. I remember attending a funeral with her of a woman who had died young, from cancer. Much was made of this woman's career, but little of her life as a mother and wife. "That other stuff doesn't mean anything, Linny," my mother said angrily outside the church. "Who she was, that's what counts."

I would like to quote one of the letters. I love this not only because it so aptly captures my mother's gentleness and softness, but because on the original hand-written version, a solitary teardrop stains the page. The writer is Timothy Findley:

Dear Murray,

Bill Whitehead and I want to extend our condolences to you and to the children at this sad time. Barbara's death was — as all deaths are — a shock, but not a shock in the wider sense. How wonderfully well she persisted and fought back. The example of that perseverance and courage is a gift she left for all of us.

Before I knew her, she interviewed me for *The Journal* in the early 1980s. I think we had met in a corridor at Film Arts and one or two "events" — but I had no real sense of knowing her beyond her public persona. When we did this interview I called her "Mrs. Frum", which I think sort of took her by surprise because everyone else called her "Barbara" on air. I was only being polite — but we laughed about it later. It wasn't until our third or fourth interview that I called her "Barbara" on air and she burst out laughing. It was lovely.

When I worked at Casey House as a volunteer (as did Bill) she came on more than one occasion to see one of her friends who was dying there. She brought a lot of strength to that place. You know this — and her friends know it — but her tireless efforts and her caring were spread over a wide perspective and, while she eschewed credit for it, she deserves it. She was, endlessly, a good woman.

My private sense of Barbara is shored and kept safe in one moment. We walked in your garden. We were part way down the hill and she stopped and looked at it and she said — very quietly — "This is my personal haven. It saves me over and over. ..." Now I think of her in that moment and I am certain she is there — still and safe.

My best to you. Tiff

There is a line from Dylan Thomas's poem "Fern Hill" that we used as an epitaph on the programs for my mother's memorial service:

> *Time held me green and dying*
> *Though I sang in my chains like the sea.*

I want to tell the songs my mother sang.

Jacob Rosberg in front of his store in the forties

Chapter 1

The Canadian Future

BARBARA FRUM:

  Do you have a wife? Do you have a personal life?

JACKIE MASON:

  I was never married.

BARBARA FRUM:

  Never married?

JACKIE MASON:

  No. I do these shows. I keep meeting girls like you and then whatever happens is nobody's business. Are you Jewish?

BARBARA FRUM:

  Yes.

JACKIE MASON:

  Oh you are! Well, how do you do. See you at four o'clock?

AS IT HAPPENS, *February 1977*

My MOTHER'S FATHER, Chaim Wronsberg, emigrated to Canada from the Czarist Empire in 1913, at age nine, along with his entire extended family of more than fifty people. Their boat docked in Quebec City, and they came by train to Toronto. Their first home was on Elizabeth Street, between College and Dundas, in the old St. John's Ward, a nineteenth-century shanty town. Elizabeth Street became the location of the Toronto General Hospital, and thus the street on which my mother died.

I first learned the story of my mother's family's arrival in Canada from a volume of family history my mother produced with the help of my brother David in the last years of her life. My mother had a consuming interest in history, in the dead. She collected hundreds of photographs of her ancestors, and went to great lengths to uncover the stories hidden beneath them. She hunted down distant relatives across North America, and persuaded my father to make a wintertime pilgrimage to Poland so that she could see the street in the village of Kielce where her father was born. (Kielce became notorious when the village's inhabitants violently attacked Jewish death camp survivors returning to their homes in the fall of 1945.)

My father would tease her, "Barbara, of all the things you could be doing with your time, why are you spending hours on the telephone tracking down your meshuggine relatives?" But there was no arguing. She was motivated not only by a love for these people and their stories, both sweet and unsavoury (she delighted in the discovery of an inept bootlegger on her mother's side of the family), but also by a sense of panic that without her efforts, these lives would slip away, lost and forgotten by the ungrateful generations that followed.

Chaim Wronsberg's father, an easy-going, modest man named Jacob, listed his occupation on his immigration papers as "labourer". His spitfire wife, Mindel, whose resources were no greater, grandly proclaimed herself to be "in business", a neat summation of her ambitious and proud personality. On arrival in Canada, somebody — probably an immigration official — changed the family name to "Rosberg", a curious spelling for a name that would soon be pronounced "Ross-berg".

Within months, the Rosberg family parted from the rest of the Wronsberg clan, and landed on a farm in Nobleton, Ontario. None of them had a shred of talent for farming. Later they could laugh at the memory of Harold, as Chaim was renamed, and his brother Joe attempting to coax a horse up a ladder; or the first winter subsisting on nothing but potatoes left in the field by the last tenant. Yet, for two difficult and frightening years, the family depended largely on the generosity of their neighbours.

It was in 1915, when their farmhouse was struck by lightning and burnt to the ground that Jacob and Mindel became convinced that they were not cut out for farming. They bought a grocery store in Toronto, on Queen Street West. The store was a modest success but Jacob, undoubtedly urged on by his wife, continued to seek out better opportunities. He found them in the construction of the Welland Canal.

Jacob Rosberg packed two suitcases of work clothes, and went to the work-site to peddle these to the labourers. His ability to converse in Polish and Russian was a great asset, and his merchandise was snapped up quickly. He returned with more, this time not just overalls, but also expensive silk shirts. After several successful selling trips, the Rosbergs saw that their future lay in clothing.

Family lore has it that Jacob chose Niagara Falls as a place to live because he noticed a large number of churches and banks from the train. As Florence Rosberg, his future daughter-in-law, remembers it, "Jacob figured it must be a nice, respectable town, full of good, pious people. And there must be a lot of money because otherwise what would they need all those banks for?"

In 1919, he opened a men's clothing store named Rosberg's at the corner of Queen and Erie, the heart of Niagara Falls' downtown. The family lived in an apartment behind the store. The store succeeded immediately, and Jacob and Mindel soon began selling ladies' and children's clothing too. For the next five decades, their department store was a fixture of the Niagara Falls shopping district. It never moved from its original location, but a series of renovations expanded the store from its original 2,000 square feet to an eventual 60,000, with space for clothing, shoes, toys, cosmetics, furniture, and appliances. A second Rosberg's was later opened in the nearby town of Welland. Rosberg's became an important institution, not only because it grew large enough to give credit and cash cheques, but because Jacob — remembering his family's own experiences — was responsive to appeals from needy families, beginning the family tradition of quiet philanthropy. Jacob was kind on principle, his son Harold was kind by instinct and nature.

My mother's father, Harold, the third of four children, was the first-born son and thus greatly favoured. His mother, Mindel, the true driving force behind the store, cherished her handsome, capable son above all others, including her husband. She would often pretend to be asleep when her husband or the other children approached, but if Harold walked in she sprang to attention. In time the store passed into his hands, but this favouritism came at a price: Harold was obliged to leave school after the eighth grade to work, a deficiency he was keenly aware of for the rest of his life.

Margaret Faiad, a sales clerk who worked at Rosberg's all her adult life, remembers: "When the store was busy Harold would do everything and anything — nothing was too low or menial. He'd bring up merchandise from the shipping room, pack bags, ring up sales. Harold could get things done just with a smile and his sweet manner."

Jacob was a hard worker, but Harold had the entrepreneurial touch. When the mayor's wife needed a dress to meet the Queen, she described what she needed to Harold and trusted him to order something just right. On a grander scale than his father, Harold donated clothing to the needy. Leadership of the Jewish merchants of the Niagara region fell naturally to him. He made a visit to one

Jewish store owner in St. Catharines, ordering the man to remove a misleading sign in his window which read, "Going Out ('for' in tiny letters) Business!" lest the deceptive sign would tarnish the integrity of the whole community. In the late thirties, he energetically organized a boycott of German goods.

Within a generation, my mother's family had been catapulted from dirt poverty in a Polish ghetto to a bountiful life in Canada. By the time my mother was born, the Rosbergs had become prominent in town, but she was always aware of her family's origins. As she once said: "I am no respecter of place at all...I've always despised the interviewer who will kick around Joe Shlunk over there and let a cabinet minister walk in and it's 'How do you do sir, such a privilege to meet you sir.' I just can't bear that [because of] the situation in which I grew up."

That situation included vivid memories of the much-less-successful New World experience of her mother's family. My mother's mother, Florence Hirschowitz, was born in a Bronx tenement in 1913. Florence's father Leo had met her mother, Dora Abramowitz, after they had arrived in the United States from opposite ends of Russia: the Baltic Coast, and Odessa on the Black Sea. They met on New York's Lower East Side and promptly married. In 1917, the young Hirschowitz family fled to Niagara Falls, New York to escape a polio epidemic then raging in the city. They did not prosper. They opened a ladies' wear store, but lost it during the depression. Humiliated, Leo took on a string of jobs. Although it was a tremendous financial burden on the family, my academically gifted grandmother entered the University of Michigan in the fall of 1931.

Days before Florence's departure for her freshman year in Ann Arbor, she and Harold met at a friend's eighteenth birthday party on the American side of the Niagara Falls border. My grandmother, the great romantic of our family, still talks with girlish passion about the moment she met him: "The minute I heard his voice, I knew I wouldn't love anybody else. I wouldn't want anybody else. That was it." There was time for only one date before she left but she and Harold promised to correspond. Most of their courtship was conducted through letters, all of which my grandmother burned as soon as her children were old enough to read them.

Florence's empathy, charm, and erudition have made her a wonderful correspondent all her life.

If Florence wrote dazzling letters, Harold cut a dazzling figure. Despite the depression, he drove an expensive Auburn roadster. The car's appearance in Ann Arbor, my grandmother remembers, "electrified everybody." Harold modestly explained that he could afford such a car because the depression in Canada wasn't as bad as it was in the United States.

"Canadians are slower about everything," he told her seductively.

Harold was handsome, suave, rich, and worldly. My grandmother, a great beauty, but terribly self-conscious because perpetually overweight, compensated with intelligence, humour, and a zest for life. She consumed cigarettes, martinis, clothes and, most of all, books, with relish. She remains one of the world's great talkers.

After she graduated from Michigan with a B.A. in English, she and Harold were married. She happily moved to Canada — a place she had only ever considered as a convenient escape from the noise of firecrackers on the Fourth of July. To this day she retains her American citizenship. For an intellectual like my grandmother, Niagara Falls was not exactly Mecca. But she was in love, and she adjusted. She worked in the store as the buyer for ladies' apparel, making frequent trips to Toronto and Montreal. And she organized a beautiful home. Eventually she would harness her energy to become the pre-eminent hostess of the Niagara Falls Jewish community, giving wonderful dinners, and arranging seminars and reading groups for her friends (as, at eighty-two years of age and a resident of Toronto, she still does).

My mother grew up with one set of grandparents on each side

of the border but it was to her affectionate, American grandparents that she felt most devoted. Florence's mother, one of six sisters, was the head of a large brood of Abramowitz cousins — whom my mother adored. "The first boy I ever had a crush on," my mother once told me, "was my cousin Harvey from Chicago. And I had another cousin who worked for the American military developing nuclear weapons. I grew up thinking these American cousins were the bravest, cleverest, most intriguing people in the world." Thus she was immunized against the emotional and irrational anti-Americanism that often plagues the Canadian media.

In 1937, when Florence became pregnant with my mother, her first child, she wanted to bless the baby with what she believed was the greatest legacy in the world: American citizenship. She had arranged to give birth on the American side of the border, at Memorial Hospital in Niagara Falls, New York. This turned out to be more difficult than Florence had planned, since she went into labour on the Jewish New Year, Rosh Hashanah. Jewish law forbids driving on holy days. Florence was never deeply religious, but out of deference to the more conservative Rosbergs she had no choice but to walk to the hospital.

Arriving at the hospital, Florence placed herself in the care of her long-time family physician. Although she had been a patient of his most of her life, Florence was unaware of his record of obstetrical incompetence. My mother was a large baby at birth, almost nine pounds. The doctor, whose weakness stemmed less from stupidity than excessive identification with the suffering of mothers, attempted his usual remedy for long and difficult labours: removal of the baby with forceps. Delivering too hastily, his metal contraption gripped my mother's right shoulder, tearing her deltoid muscle (the muscle that controls the arm's movement). Florence was later to discover that this was a trademark delivery of this doctor and that some of his infant patients had died this way.

When her daughter was brought to Florence for the first time, the baby's arm was in a sling safety-pinned to a gauze band around her forehead. "She looked like Pocahontas saluting the marines," Florence remembers.

With neither apology nor self-reproach, the doctor told her there had been a birth injury, and did not mention that the baby's disability would be permanent.

Florence and Harold always minimized that disability. They thought it a temporary problem, not a devastating loss, nor an act of malpractice requiring recriminations.

My mother wore a metal and leather corset day and night for the first three years of her life. The corset was worn laced up to her body, with a metal brace angled in such a way as to keep her arm propped up, as though she were making a right-hand turn signal but with her palm facing skyward. It would be an uncomfortable position for anyone, let alone a baby, and it made her awkward to cuddle.

If it is true that an individual's character is formed in the first three years of life, this is when my mother learned to bear her burdens gallantly. Florence never indulged her daughter with pity or fuss, nor did she allow others to. She had no time for the "victim mentality".

"It wouldn't surprise me if Barbara thought all kids came out that way," Florence says. "I never allowed her to think that she was abnormal or unequal to whatever was expected of her."

The first jab of reality my mother faced on the subject of her handicap came at age four and a half, when Suzy was born. Staring at her baby sister, born not only without abnormalities but also prettier and cuter, she said despondently, "Ma, you said that everyone has something wrong with them. But what's wrong with her? She looks perfect to me."

Looking down at the exquisite baby in her arms, Florence

comforted her sad, elder daughter. "Barbara, I assure you, no one's life is perfect. Everyone has a turn. Only the timing is different."

One of Suzy's earliest memories is of her nine-year-old sister going to the basement every morning for physical therapy. "A woman would come to the house to work with her. I thought it was a terrible burden for her, but she seemed courageous about it."

My mother's early education was all aimed at helping to correct the problems of her arm and hand. She was started on piano lessons at age four. She got to and from these lessons by herself, on the Lundy's Lane streetcar. When the streetcar arrived at the right stop, the conductor escorted tiny Barbara across the street to the piano teacher's house while the other passengers waited.

When she was not at piano lessons, dance lessons, or in physical therapy, my mother would go with Florence to Rosberg's store. "We would walk into the men's department and go straight to the back," my grandmother remembers. "I put her on top of the desk where Uncle Joe did the cash and I would sit there reading her stories. My favourite story to read to her was the story that I always felt was the theme of my psyche: *The Ugly Duckling*. And what was fantastic was that I would read it to Barbara who would always cry at exactly the right place. She loved that story. It may have been the theme of her psyche too."

As an adult, my mother became adept at hiding her disability. It was something others had to notice on their own. A high school friend who travelled with her on a cross-country bike trip thirty-five years ago still remembers becoming annoyed because of the laborious way she rolled her sleeping bag and packed her knapsack.

"Honestly Barbara," she snapped. "You'd think there was something wrong with your arm!"

"There is," my mother told her calmly. That was all she said.

When driving, my mother had to reach across her body with her left arm to shift gears. In the first year of her marriage to my father, she smashed up his new Oldsmobile by driving it into the wall of their apartment building garage. She was unable to turn the garage key, steer, and change gears in the same motion, as required.

Few understood the reason for her distinctive, left-handed handshake. People were usually touched that she appeared to want to hold their hand with her left hand, rather than shake it with her right. They didn't know she could not do otherwise. It was a subtle contribution, I believe, to the common perception of her personal warmth.

My mother could not run because she could not co-ordinate her arms to keep balance. And yet, she was graceful. Watching her tend her garden or cuddle a baby, it was impossible to think that she was disabled.

Both Suzy and I are left-handed, and my mother may have been programmed that way too. But I doubt it: she didn't have any of the flaky characteristics one normally associates with lefties. And for a perfectionist, her handwriting was oddly sloppy. But then again, a handwriting expert from the *Toronto Star* once analyzed an anonymous sample of it and pronounced that "it communicates a definite spiritual feeling." The expert said the author possessed "great perseverance" and was "very determined". She "switches from being quite talkative to closing people out and tends to be secretive about herself." All of which was true, so maybe my mother was a natural lefty after all.

Florence succeeded in persuading my mother that she was blessed and capable. As my mother's close friend Geraldine Sherman observes: "Barbara's body was not equal to her mind. She was not a dancer. She didn't have that rhythm or easiness with her body. But she could dance with her mind. She may have recognized even as a child that this body that she had been given was not equal to her mind. There was an imbalance right from the beginning."

Barbara at age four

Chapter 2

A Respected Child

BARBARA FRUM:

> Miss Bhutto, will you answer in a simple sentence how much
> are you your father's daughter? How much are you fulfilling
> his ambition for you now?

BENAZIR BHUTTO:

> I think my father would be very angry with me if he ever
> thought that I was doing what I was doing for him. He
> would want me to do what I am doing for my country.
> And I hope that I am doing what I am doing for my coun-
> try, and thereby, in a way, paying tribute to him, too.

> THE JOURNAL, *September 1986*

THE GARISH NIAGARA FALLS of today bears little resemblance
to the Niagara Falls of my mother's youth. The wax museums,
haunted houses, mini-golf courses, IMAX theatre, and pancake
palaces arrived in the seventies. On the visits my brother David and
I made as children, we watched with wide-eyed enthusiasm as the
town was transformed from tourist attraction to trap.

We greeted with particular glee the construction of a grey and
neon-pink hamburger stand in the shape of a flying saucer at the

corner where our grandmother's quiet street met the main drag, and were baffled by her horror. We were never allowed to eat there, desperately though we wanted to. Such architectural atrocities, which helped drive my grandmother to Toronto in 1977, could hardly have been imagined when my mother was young. Her Niagara Falls was a subdued factory town, with a modest business community, a single strip of flashy motels, and one spectacular force of nature. It was a safe, solid town that revered work and practised honesty.

My mother seldom encountered the anti-Semitism that my father grew up with in the Toronto of the thirties. The Niagara Falls Jewish community was small but welcomed. In an act of true decency, a portion of the historic town cemetery was sold to the synagogue to create a separate Jewish burial ground, as required by Jewish law. That kindliness in turn bred respect in my mother. Years later, when I brought home a string of WASP boyfriends, she would rationalize her Jewish-mother disappointment by saying with great sincerity: "Well, it *was* his ancestors who built this great country..."

It was a town where everyone knew each other. A block from Corwin Avenue, my mother's street, lived the aptly-named Mr. Pew, whose garden of green onions and garlic was regularly raided by the neighbourhood children. Eleanor, the neighbourhood bully, lived across the street. She tormented my mother by dropping frogs down her dress, and, in one character-forming encounter, offered a piece of fudge that turned out to be shoe polish. A few houses away lived the prettiest girl in town, Laura Sauer, whom my mother's brother Gerry married after graduating from college, though it is certain he first proposed no later than grade eight.

"I felt the whole street was my family," my mother once said. "When you grew up in the Falls you weren't just raised in your own house. It was as if the whole community had a vested interest in you. ... I remember once going to high school in grade nine and this wonderful woman came out of her house with an umbrella. She said, 'Dear, you're going to be soaking wet by the time you get to the collegiate. You just bring it back to me on your way home.' ... I was very young and that formed me."

But while Niagara Falls nurtured and coddled and stamped her with its admirable values, its toxins may have poisoned her. Perhaps it was the electro-magnetic fields which surround the Falls, or the cyanide plant a few miles from her home, or the chemical industries of Love Canal, just across the river, which made my mother one of Niagara Falls' disproportionately numerous cancer victims.

David was five and I was three when my mother first put us on a Grey Coach bus to the Falls by ourselves. My parents would introduce us to the driver and seat us in the front row. The minute we were unloaded at the Niagara Falls depot, we would fly into Florence's arms. We adored her for many reasons not least of which was because she wanted us to call her Florence. We didn't know anyone who called a grandmother by her first name.

After our long bus trip, Florence would drive us immediately to Rosberg's. This was no idle call. Probably through the giddy joy of seeing us off, our mother would usually neglect to pack clothing. All we took was a green vinyl bag which we ourselves filled with books and toys. Eventually, Florence came to expect this, and scheduled the scooping up of a weekend's supply of play clothes, toothbrushes, and pajamas. The Rosberg's staff, many of them lifetime employees, would gush over us.

"Barbara's kids?" they would chuckle, and shower effusive praise.

David and I were awed by the grandeur of Rosberg's, *circa* 1968, before our grandfather's death, cross-border shopping and suburban super-malls left the store in decline. Our comparison was the small Toronto convenience store on College Street owned by our father's parents. There, we would blissfully gorge on potato chips and 7-Up while our Zaydie, perched atop a packing-crate filled with paper towels, fashioned sailboat hats from the newspapers he used to wrap groceries.

We thought that was swell. But if the College Street store was a little paradise, Rosberg's was the miracle on Thirty-fourth Street. Of course, the whole of Rosberg's could probably have fit into Macy's sporting-goods department, but we hadn't seen that. Harold's office was grand and dark, at least in memory, with an enormous antique globe in one corner. It seemed he was attending to great affairs of state, as powerful as J. P. Morgan.

None of his affairs mattered more than his grandchildren. One foggy night, after seating David and me on the bus back to Toronto, he commanded the driver to "wait right there." He ran to the men's room, emerging with a handful of wet paper towels, and wiped the bus's offending headlights clean. Nodding to the driver, he ordered: "Okay, now you can go."

We may have misjudged the scope of his jurisdiction, but we accurately assessed his goodness. Harold Rosberg was gentle and affectionate with his grandchildren, just as he had been with his own children. On birthdays and at Chanukah, he could be counted on to supply the most exciting presents, bravely defying our parents' interdiction against "commercial, plastic toys." The party did not begin until Harold arrived with a Hot Wheels racing track, a gaudy Mattel doll, or a Man From Uncle briefcase complete with toy Luger.

My grandparents lived in an elegant, Georgian-style, four-bedroom home built in 1942. Although actually rather modest in size, it ranked in our young eyes as one of the stately homes of Canada, its colonnaded front vastly more impressive than the functional, modernist bungalow we lived in. The one-acre lot on which the house stood seemed like a garden from an A. A. Milne story, with velvety lawns, thick fruit orchards, and an intoxicating rose garden bordered on three sides by neatly trimmed hedges. A small swimming pool was dug in the sixties.

My mother believed that it is through smell that we relive memories. My grandparents' house was filled with the pungent smell of delicacies cooked by Eva Baller, their beloved housekeeper. Eva was a German communist from Slovenia, utterly dedicated to the wealthy, Jewish family she served for thirty years. Eva's bedroom, shared with her toy poodle Fifi, was located on the second floor with all the other bedrooms. Gerry remembers that the house had two factions: the adults — Florence, Harold, and Barbara — and the kids — Suzy and Gerry, captained by Eva.

A gifted cook, Eva was an absolutely brilliant baker, famous for her hand-rolled apricot cookies and crispy fried chicken. The aromas of her kitchen were enhanced by the perfume of peaches, cherries, apricots, and plums plucked fresh from Florence's orchard. In the basement, refrigerators and freezers overflowed with cookies, pies, and preserves; the many shelves were stacked high with cans of black olives and tuna fish.

Eva kept the house pristine. The golden silk fabric covering the sofas was never creased, and vacuum lines were visible in the wall to wall carpet. Hand towels in the bathroom were stiffly starched and ironed into alignment, so that one couldn't bear to use them. Scattered about the house were never-empty cigarette boxes paired with *objet d'art* cigarette lighters so heavy even adults required two hands. The library was filled with rows of splendid books — Poe, Sherlock Holmes, Dumas, three or four different translations of Homer. There was one shelf for the Greek dramatists and another for innumerable editions of Shakespeare.

The uncompromising order of the house was not something Florence indulged only after the departure of her children. She had never wished "to live in a kindergarten", as she said. When my mother was a girl, breakfast was not served until she had dressed and made her bed. And that bed had a complex, green velvet bedspread, with skirts folded into three parts. If the pillow didn't fold in "just so", it had to be done again. Once the bed was made, it could not be sat on — certainly not sprawled on! — until bedtime. Homework was completed upright, at a desk in the bedroom, the only exception being exam time, when, in deference to summer heat, studying was allowed on the screened back porch.

After school, my mother was obliged to take her books and belongings directly to her room. If personal items were not put in their proper place, Florence hid them. Once when her brother lost something, my mother advised him drily, "Gerry, look in the freezer. She puts everything in there, including umbrellas."

"Part of my mother's rules," remembers Suzy, "was that there was no way Eva should be expected to clean up our mess. One of my best tricks was when I tried something on and I didn't want to wear it, I threw it in the corner, for the laundry, so that I didn't have to hang it up again. When my mother found out I was prepared to make work for Eva because I was lazy, she was outraged. She considered it a despicable thing to do."

Eva's day was busy enough assisting Florence with one of her primary occupations: entertaining. Visitors poured in and out of the Rosberg house; a steady stream of family and friends, traveling Jewish salesmen, representatives of B'nai Brith and other Jewish organizations, and, on one memorable occasion, the fifty members of the all-black, all-male Norman De Paur Infantry Chorus.

In the words of my Aunt Suzy, "Florence was a lady high on stylistics. She had the flair for it." Reality unfortunately did not always accommodate her aspirations. She had installed a foot-buzzer by her chair in the dining room, an ingenious method of silently summoning Eva to clear plates between courses. But Eva, who had read fewer nineteenth-century novels than Florence, would undo her, poking her head from behind the kitchen door to bellow: "What you want Missus?!"

Eva was not the only one ever to bristle against Florence's

standards. After a party for which my twelve-year-old mother had been conscripted as dish-washer, she carped from behind a stack of dirty dessert bowls: "Mother, if you needed more servants you should have had more children!"

The standards were relaxed for Florence's grandchildren, and my mother did not even come close to replicating them in her own house. Which doesn't mean I couldn't appreciate the sensuality of a Corwin Avenue bed. Underneath the heavy, luxurious velvet cover were satiny cotton bed sheets, cool and smooth as ice cream. Lying in my mother's bed, I would try to imagine what kind of little girl she had been, to the extent that any child can imagine her parents to have been children themselves. Doubly puzzling in my case, for my mother never really believed she was a child. "I was born an adult," she would often say. She believed that some people were born with "old souls". Everyone who knew her agreed.

"She was never a child," Suzy tells me now. "In some funny way, she was the most stable one in the home. She's the only five-year-old I've ever known that everybody respected.

Happy though her family was, photographs of my mother as a young girl show her with a serious expression verging on melancholy. It was as though she knew she must always be, in Suzy's words, "the elder".

Florence says: "Barbara was old beyond her years. What was forced on her was excessive responsibility and maturity. We had such high standards for her and she bought right into them. She never protested. I wasn't bringing up a little kid, I was bringing up a best friend. She couldn't twitch a muscle that wasn't subject to scrutiny. It should have had a very bad result."

Florence has always judged herself severely. In fact, all three of her children achieved great success. Suzy raised four children, founded and operated the muffin and cookie chain Treats, and is now completing a doctorate. Gerry, graduated from Harvard College and Harvard Law School, clerked for U.S. Supreme Court Justice William Brennan and worked at the State Department, before flourishing in the computer software industry. He is now an executive at the *Washington Post*. But it was Barbara who was the chief focus of Florence's intense, intellectual mothering, because, as my grandmother explains, it was Barbara who was most like Florence. In her first-born, Florence saw a younger version of herself: a sharp, sassy, opinionated girl, and she set out to give her the kind of education she knew such a person needed.

"I tried to be the mother that I had wanted," my grandmother explains. "From the time she was three years old, I treated Barbara as though she were an adult my age. Barbara would ask questions about everything and I'd answer her as though she were a Philadelphia lawyer. It's like the joke Trent Frayne used to tell about David when he was a little kid, 'Who's that midget the Frums invite to all their parties?' That's what Barbara was like.

"When she made a mess with her toys you could never just say to this three-year-old: 'Clean that up!' She would ask, 'Why?' It would never occur to me to say, 'Because I said so!' First you had to answer all her questions, which I guess was fair enough. But if you didn't give her answers, you would be driven out of your mind. Everywhere we went she would ask: 'What's this for?' 'Why is she doing that?' 'What are you doing?' You had to answer every question or she would embarrass you. If you ignored her, she was not above going to the upstairs window and yelling: 'My mother treats me terrible. My mother's mean. I think she's my step-mother.' That kind of thing."

Even my grandfather Harold, who was indefatigably good-natured, used to exclaim in exasperation: "Barbara, why don't you wait for the answer before you ask another question?"

When my mother was six years old, she somehow embraced the idea that life would not be complete without a pony. Florence knew a simple "no" would not suffice. She painstakingly explained why it wasn't possible, resting her case on the claim that the neighbours wouldn't like it.

"I see," replied my mother.

Soon she returned to Florence with a petition she had drafted, bearing the signatures of everyone on Corwin Avenue.

"I've asked them," my mother explained, "and none of them mind if I have a pony."

Exhausting though it was, Florence encouraged my mother's independence. By her sixth birthday, Barbara had accumulated enough gift money that Florence decided it was time for her to have her own account, and she took her to the family bank.

"I asked the manager to show her what he was going to do with her money," my grandmother says. "I wanted him to show her the big safes so she knew her money would be safe — this whole fifty dollars we were bringing in there. After he gave her the tour he said to me jokingly, 'Of course, if she ever comes in here and tries to cash out, I'll call you first.' And I said, 'You'll be doing something very wrong if you do that. This is her money and the only one who can tell you what to do with it is Barbara.'"

I glimpse the kind of mother my grandmother must have been when I see her with my own young children. She has also opened bank accounts in their names (no tour yet), and although they can't read, they already have their own library cards. When the kids reached eighteen months of age, she initiated weekly lunches at the Park Plaza Hotel in a — so far fruitless — attempt to refine their dining manners. She hands me baby-advice books, with passages underlined. Once she brought a plastic bread-box filled with large wooden beads. At the sight of this treasure, my children, and David's, who were visiting at the time, threw aside their Fisher Price farm, their trucks, and their boring-but-good-for-you Dutch educational toys, to run fingers through the beads, and listen as they cascaded across the floor.

Florence poured herself into Barbara. Or rather, poured Barbara into her own mould. She read to her constantly until my mother could read herself. She enrolled my mother in every imaginable stimulating program, and dressed her in exquisite clothing of Florence's own design. "If I went out looking like Mrs. Astor's pet horse," my grandmother says, "I couldn't see dressing my child as though she had shopped at the Salvation Army. In other words, whatever was good for us, was always the way for our kids. So if we travelled, they did. If we wore expensive clothes, so did they. Age had nothing to do with it."

Florence admits that her standards for Barbara must sometimes have been an unwanted burden. "One time, Suzy picked up a Belleek candy dish in the living room and threw it over her shoulder. It cracked into fifty million little splinters. And I said, 'Oh my goodness!' And Barbara said, 'If I'd done that, you wouldn't have just said, "Oh my goodness!"' And she was right. I would have screamed."

With such pressure on my mother, her sister Suzy has few memories of the two of them just goofing around. "I can remember the few times that we did really laugh and giggle because they seemed so exceptional. Like the night when I finally got her to play 'Who do you like better?' The game was that you would lie in bed and ask: who do you like better, Sally or Sandra? Cousin Judy or Cousin Debby? And then you'd start getting dangerous — who do you like better Mummy or Daddy? Everybody liked this game and thought it was funny, except Barbara. One day I trapped her and she gave me an answer. When we both realized that she had given me an answer, we both got hysterical, just hysterical."

But so too was she gentle and sweet. In home movies with her two siblings, she wraps her arms around them, or turns their gaze away from her towards the camera. Her tenderness towards her much younger brother is evident in a letter she wrote to Florence and Harold from a summer camp where she was a teenage counsellor and Gerry a camper:

> Gerry was so adorable last night, I could have eaten him
> up. I stopped by at his cabin at eleven o'clock, just as they
> were taking him to the bathroom. You know what Kootser's
> like when you pull him out of bed. Anyway, when he got
> back in I sat down beside him and straightened his sheet.
> "Kootsie," I said, "do you know who this is?" He opened
> one eye, looked at me for a minute and said, "Mommy?"
> He was so cute. I gave him a great big kiss from both of
> you before he fell asleep again.

Although discipline was at the core of her childhood, my mother also enjoyed an ease, peace and predictability hard to imagine today. Her father would walk in the door precisely at 6:30 every night. He never had to stay late, he never brought work home with him. Moments after his arrival, Eva served a dinner of meat and potatoes and the family exchanged their news of the day. With rules there is simplicity; with simplicity, happiness.

Barbara, Harold, Suzy in 1951

Chapter 3

Growth and Movement

BARBARA FRUM:

Maharishi, it's been delightful to talk to you.

MAHARISHI MAHESH YOGI:

And all my love and great greetings to the whole population of Canada...

BARBARA FRUM:

Fantastic. Thank you very much.

MAHARISHI MAHESH YOGI:

It's beautiful.

BARBARA FRUM:

How come you're so happy?

MAHARISHI MAHESH YOGI:

It's natural. It's the nature of life. Life is bliss.

BARBARA FRUM:

I must remember that, Maharishi.

MAHARISHI MAHESH YOGI:

Life is bliss.

BARBARA FRUM:

I must remember that.

AS IT HAPPENS, *March 1975*

IT WAS MY GRANDMOTHER's philosophy that every minute in a young woman's life should be devoted to "growth". It was also part of her philosophy that growth needn't result from happiness; just as often it could be the product of misery. Which is not to say that she wished her daughter miserable, but that happiness in itself was not held to be a prerequisite for a well-spent youth.

My mother's adolescence was not miserable, though perhaps it was lonely. As I started to research this book, I asked my grandmother for the name of my mother's best friend in high school. She gave it, and I realized I had never heard this woman's name before. I called her and she agreed to meet me at her home near Niagara Falls. After a few embarrassing minutes, it became clear that though she wished to help, she could offer no insights or anecdotes. My mother and her best high school friend were never close.

My mother certainly seemed popular and happy in high school: she was selected as valedictorian (an honour awarded at Stamford Collegiate to the student with the best character, not necessarily the best marks), and elected student council president. But her main source of companionship during those years remained her mother. My Aunt Suzy remembers coming home from school, and seeing Barbara, already home, in conversation with Florence in the book-lined den. They were so undistractable that Suzy wouldn't even stop to say hello. "Barbara's intellectual partnership with our mother was extremely strong," Suzy remembers. "Florence paid her wonderful intellectual tribute."

My mother was one of a handful of Jewish students at the oldest high school in the town, but that was not the reason for her isolation. "I didn't have a sense that she was set apart because she was Jewish," her friend told me. "I had a sense that she was different. Maybe because her mother didn't let her do certain things. Or maybe because she was more mature. She was not interested in the boys in her class."

She was not particularly interested in *anyone* in her class. She didn't spend her evenings on the telephone, but socialized with her parents and their friends. She needed to put great efforts into her studies, for she was not a natural scholar. As she would later say about herself, "I'm the kind of student who got E for effort more than A for aptitude." She told writer Heather Robertson: "My parents didn't demand that I be brilliant. I always used to win the effort awards. 'You're a plugger, make the most of your gifts.' I used to enter oratorical contests at school. One part of me would volunteer — and then the panic! My parents wouldn't let me back out. 'You stay in. You can't quit. It's good for you!' The contests used to be held on parents' night, with eight hundred people sitting out there in the auditorium. It was exquisite agony — and I used to win. I'd be in the money. You learn something from that."

"People expected a lot of me," she told Robertson. "They made incredible demands of me. It was because my father was one of the wealthiest men in a small town. He was painfully shy but he sat on committees and forced himself to make speeches at meetings. It was *noblesse oblige.* I was very conscious of that. Always I was a complete outsider. 'You're different,' people would say. I remember at school one day standing around with a bunch of my friends, chewing gum. A teacher came down the hall and said, 'Oh Barbara, not you!'"

(My mother never stopped trying to please her mother. It was Florence she called immediately after the first broadcast of *The Journal,* eager for her reaction. Florence responded by sending my mother a bouquet of flowers, with a card that read: "To the woman I would most like to emulate".)

But Florence insists that it was my mother herself, more than anyone, who pushed for academic success. "Barbara once failed a German exam in the ninth or tenth grade," my grandmother says. "You *knew* it would never happen to her again."

Her Grade Ten Proficiency Award was a copy of *Emily Post's Guide to Etiquette*, which, having survived forty years of spring cleanings, was clearly cherished. I can imagine my mother as a teenager, reading Post's rules of proper conduct between men and women in dating and marriage, and accepting them as sensible and right. "Everything that shows a lack of courtesy toward others is rude." "If you would be thought likable, don't nudge or paw or finger people." "Don't hold hands or walk arm-about-waist in public." "Don't allow anyone to paw you." (My mother hated to be hugged or kissed by social acquaintances.)

As my mother grew older, her need for independence from Florence's strong influence led to some friction. Florence, for example, was dead set against my mother's wishes to join a high school sorority, explaining that, "the sorority was an organization built for snobs and that therefore it was not her kind of thing." My mother insisted on joining one anyway. It was a strangely out-of-character desire, but I think I can understand it. When you are the only Jewish girl in your class, you need to know that you can fit in, even if later you choose not to.

"She went through a horrendous rush period doing all the goofy things," remembers my grandmother, "wearing make-up on half of her face and putting her clothes on backwards. But when it came time to pick the next group of girls the following year, she said she was going to quit. Why? Because she couldn't participate in the stupidity and the cruelty they were showing the new girls. She hated it and she didn't approve. As much as I hadn't wanted her to join the sorority in the first place, now I told her she couldn't quit because she had made a commitment and she had to stay. If she didn't like the sorority, the only way out was to change it. Quitting was absolutely not allowed." She did not quit.

Florence demanded that each of my mother's summers had to be an adventure. Florence did not permit any of her children to work in the store. "I didn't want them in there with Mindel boss-ing them around all day." They had to spend their time doing something "educational". My mother went to camp, travelled, or studied. And once the activity was selected, usually by Florence, there was no way out.

Misery overcame my mother during a summer at National Music Camp in Interlochen, Michigan, studying drama and oper-etta at the age of thirteen. She begged Harold and Florence to allow her to come home, but her entreaties were rejected.

"I wouldn't hear of it," says Florence. "She stayed and she was very courageous about it. The next year she went back and she was absolutely a star, a hit, and everything turned out just fine. That gave her an enormous feeling that you can go back and fix things in spades. Not only that you can, but you must." Twenty-five years later, our mother would send David and me to Interlochen too. We didn't like it any better than she had.

The summer before she turned seventeen, my mother arranged to go on a biking trip across Western Canada and the United States. It was ambitious: 3,000 miles; 1,500 on the bike. The trip, with its stops at the Grand Canyon, the Montana Badlands and Banff National Park, gave my mother a life-long appreciation of the gran-deur of nature. It also was the origin of an obsession with methodi-cal, economical packing.

The group camped in pup tents, and received lectures from park rangers in the evenings. My mother loved it, so much that, the day she suffered a serious accident, her diary gives three pages to what a fabulous time she had, before mentioning how it ended: "Our bikes had picked up quite a bit of speed…and I…was knocked off my bike. I must have been out for a few seconds but when I came to, I was laughing it off because I thought I wasn't hurt. When I saw the blood all over my clothes and body I realized that I was. By this time [a friend] had forced me to sit down with my head back and was blotting the blood on my face. I had a bad gash on the underside of my lip which made it swell up a lot so that it jutted out over my lower lip. Because I had fallen on my nose it was badly swollen too. I had bad brush burns on my left knee, left elbow and hand, right shoulder, forehead, chin, right cheek and area between nose and mouth. I looked like a real case. Both sides of my nose were badly bleeding and of course my mouth was too." No doubt the accident was caused by her bad arm and its effect on her balance, but she makes no mention of that. She probably didn't even allow herself to think it.

Luckily, Florence and Harold, who were taking a summer trip to California, had already arranged to meet up with her in Jasper. When they got there, Florence recalls, "Barbara's face looked like hamburger." The doctor in Jasper insisted that the best thing to do was to not touch her face at all. If she allowed it to form scabs, it would heal from beneath the skin. Florence, looking around at the hut that served as Jasper's hospital, was appalled. She insisted that Barbara quit the trip immediately, and come to California to see a specialist that she had contacted by telephone, who was offering a more elaborate mummification. But my mother, who had listened carefully to the Canadian doctor's analysis, decided to trust him, and overruled.

My mother knew she was taking a risk: "She had visions that after the accident she would have a scarred face, and a bad nose, as well as a bad arm. It was very traumatic," my grandmother says. But she stayed on the trip, "even though she looked, there is no other word for it, ugly." Courage overcame vanity. As reward, my mother's face healed perfectly, without a single scar. Her nose, untreated for fracture, did however, take on a slightly different shape.

The last summer of her youth, my mother returned to National Music Camp, where she awaited word of her acceptance at university. On August 12, 1955 Florence wrote:

Dear Barb,

I have just placed a phone call to you at Interlochen and while waiting for them to trace you and bring you to the phone, I've decided to start writing — just because I'm too excited to sit and wait. . . . You go to U. of T. in the Fall — and that's the biggest milestone we're going to celebrate as parents, at least so far. You will be excited, I know — and you can well believe me when I say that we are too. I never thought I'd be one of these foolish parents who harks back to "It seems like only yesterday when I was reading you A. A. Milne" — remember how I propped you way up on a counter in the store, to make sure of my audience, because you were too little to get down by yourself, and I read you and read you those poems? . . . My heart just races with excitement every time I think of the place you've made for yourself, and what equipment and character you are bringing to your future . . . I love the way you think, the manner in which you set about learning, the way your accumulated knowledge over the years has brought you a certain sweetness and wisdom, and the willingness and eagerness and faith you bring to every job. Those attributes are usually crowned with success! . . .

Entering university was both exhilarating and slightly terrifying for women of my mother's generation for reasons that have since changed. Many female students entered their freshman fall with the realistic expectation of a springtime proposal. Often women would drop out of university the moment they became engaged. Even my mother, who was seriously interested in her education, anticipated leaving university as a married woman.

"All the girls are getting married here it seems," she wrote to her mother near the end of her first year. "Probably to get out of school. Every day we hear about somebody else; I know of at least ten girls from Soc & Phil getting married in May. Esther and I are rapidly being lost in the shuffle — but we're not worried."

Esther Brown was my mother's roommate, and her first close female friend. "We told each other everything," she remembers. It was the closest bond I'd ever had with anybody." I know the same was true for my mother.

The two girls had much in common: they were both Jewish, from small Ontario towns, and the daughters of merchants. "Barbara's family was wealthier, and more settled, but she instantly put me at ease by saying 'We're just one generation ahead of you.'" It was no coincidence that they were both Jewish. University College — the "Godless College," unlike Anglican Trinity, Presbyterian Victoria, and Catholic St. Michael's, had the highest proportion of Jewish students. But according to Esther, "there were only about six Jewish girls in residence." The university ensured they lived together.

Esther vividly recalls their first meeting. Not for the last time in her life, my mother's wardrobe made a big impact. My mother was wearing sheer nylons, when most girls wore leotards. Then Florence walked into the room, "carrying a record player and a stand. They came in with a lot of stuff."

Surveying their haul, Esther discerned a problem. "I had read the rules carefully before I arrived and I knew that *nothing* was allowed. There were rules about when to go to bed. You had to sign out to go out for the evening. Twice a week you could stay out until 12:30 a.m., and once a week until 2:00 a.m. That was it. There was no music allowed. And definitely, no record players."

Esther politely explained to Florence, "I don't know if this is going to be a problem or not, but the rules say no record players."

"We'll just have to see about that," Florence replied.

"It took her about twelve minutes to have the rule changed," Esther says. With the ban on music lifted, the two girls enjoyed regular, musical serenades.

"Barbara brought Kurt Weill music. She had Smetana, Lotte Lenya. There was an Italian woman by the name of Katyna Ranieri. She sang love songs. We would put this on at night. In the morning there could be heavy music. But at night we got very romantic. We would listen to these love songs over and over again and then go to sleep."

The first night together in residence, they discussed whether or not it was fate to fall in love with one person. My romantic mother suspected so.

For the out-of-town girls of Whitney Hall residence, university was designed not only to broaden the mind, but to make a lady of you. There was a Mistress of Deportment, with whom the girls drank coffee in the drawing room after dinner. My mother encountered this woman in her first week of school. As the Mistress poured my mother a cup of coffee, she asked, in a rich Upper Canadian accent: "One lump or two?"

"Three please," replied my mother.

"One lump or two?" the Mistress repeated.

The dining room was ruled by a woman named Irene, "with an iron hand," according to Esther. "It was a very formal dining room, with second helpings offered only rarely. You walked in and stood behind your chair. Where you stood determined which job you'd have. Tables were for eight and you could sit at whichever table you wanted, but it was the job of the person at the head of the table to serve the food. The person to the right was responsible for clearing the table. When clearing you could only carry two plates at a time. You never wanted that chair.

"Barbara and I had never seen eight onions served for eight people. In our homes there had always been more food than you could ever, ever eat. We were fascinated with it. It was a completely new ball game. Dessert was served with a fork and spoon.

"Irene would let you know if second helpings were available.

She stood behind a serving table at the doorway to the kitchen and she would bring in additional food, and then, and only then, could you take your silver tray over for more. It was portioned out to the girl, to the letter.

"The first night they served pork chops with apple sauce. By the end of the night you knew who was Jewish — we eyed each other uncomfortably but we all ate our dinners."

My mother completed a four year honours B.A. in history, an ambitious degree for a woman of her generation. She was, as she had been in high school, a dedicated student, but she was not so studious as to not participate in the high-minded fun of campus life. She told the Brock University graduating class in 1987: "I joined every society, film club; I was there for every debate, play, concert and symposium. We felt ourselves on the most glamorous possible rehearsal stage for real life ahead."

Still, her most important university experiences occurred in the classroom. At a speech she gave in honour of the centennial of Toronto's History Department she said: "This place taught me — before journalism could — that there is no single truth, [a lesson that was] quite disillusioning at first, but mobilizing thereafter... It taught me that it was your *duty* to sift the evidence, search for motive, check who said it, when, in what context and did they later adjust their view. ... We learned how to read a book, as you'd read a person, and to respect it only if it was good. We learned that all ideas are not equal — and we wanted to have the quality of ideas that would earn *us* respect too.

"I am sure that the four years I laboured in the Department of History shaped my outlook and style of operating more than I even know. I was taxed to the limit — absolutely flooded out — but if the Method didn't break you, it made you a student for life. Of course you would *never catch up* — that was the point — but it left you with an appetite to struggle."

Florence Rosberg née Hirschowitz, my mother's mother.

Harold and Florence Rosberg shortly after their marriage, in Miami Beach 1935: like my mother, my grandmother made a match that was spectacularly right.

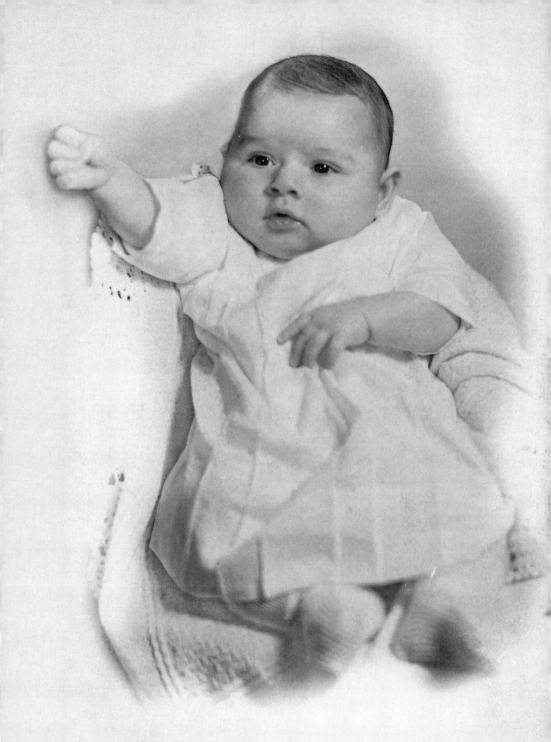

The baby Barbara Rosberg. Her right arm was disabled at birth. When she first saw her, Florence had thought she looked like "Pocahontes saluting the marines."

Barbara with Pophead in 1941; and writing to him as a teenager.

Daddy —

Happy Birthday to you now that you are fifty, I'd love to write a poem or compose a song but all I can do is say —

Thank you for your Chumah tales
I love them every time,
Thank you for your faith in me
And patience, when I'm wrong.
For taking my part if I'm losing,
and praising when I win.
For always showing interest,
In the dullest thing I did.
But most of all for loving us,
and being just plain Pophead.

Barbara

The family store in Niagara Falls; and the house my mother lived in as a child.

Florence and Harold in the gay fifties. Below, the Rosberg family portrait. Left to right: Eva Baller (the housekeeper), Barbara, Suzy (seated), Leo and Dora Hirschowitz, Florence, Gerry, and Harold.

Barbara Rosberg, Stamford Collegiate Valedictorian for 1955, shaking the hand of the University of Toronto's president, Claude Bissell; and in a less formal moment below.

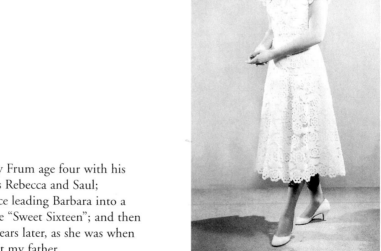

Murray Frum age four with his
parents Rebecca and Saul;
Florence leading Barbara into a
surprise "Sweet Sixteen"; and then
three years later, as she was when
she met my father.

September 3rd, 1957.

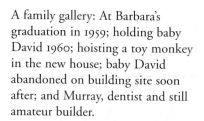

A family gallery: At Barbara's graduation in 1959; holding baby David 1960; hoisting a toy monkey in the new house; baby David abandoned on building site soon after; and Murray, dentist and still amateur builder.

Me: with Matthew, Mum and David; alone with my big brother (as adored then as now); with Mum the summer I went off to camp; and dreaming of Barbie dolls.

Wife, mother, and . . . a host of
The Day It Is, September 1968.

At work and at home:
The *As It Happens*
office, where there were
"not so much story
meetings as emergency
councils" according to
Max Allen; and below,
posed in Ron Thom's
big room.

With Alan (Lord)
Maitland (of snacks) on
air with *As It Happens*;
and below, off air, in
Jean Chretien's lap.

BARBARA
FRUM

AS IT
HAPPENED

The cover of "that damn book" which took up so much energy soon after her leukemia diagnosis. Later, she found the stress of work helped keep her alive.

By the late seventies, *As It Happens* and Barbara Frum were the same woman.
(Note the ring.)

She joked that classes in Canadian constitutional history were torture. "Stiff-stiff porridge," she called them. "But then thirty years later Meech Lake came into my life, and was I ready ladies and gentlemen? I was ready."

Florence insisted that my mother spend a summer in Europe, which was a very different sort of place in those days, still digging out from the ruin of war. Then, a single Canadian dollar could buy a tasty lunch at any bistro. My mother suggested to Esther that they make the trip together at the end of their freshman year. "We each had a travel book created by Florence," Esther remembers. "'When in London this is what you have to see...' It was our own Michelin Guide. Florence told us to take notes. She was very big on writing diaries and journals. We would write in our books before bed. It was mandatory."

Before my mother left, she and Florence had one last mother-and-child fight over my mother's preparations. My mother was still too young and inexperienced to make her own arrangements, but she was old enough to bristle at the control her mother still exerted over her life. On the boat trip across the Atlantic, my mother wrote Florence a letter to apologize; but it concluded that next time it would be better if she did everything on her own.

Florence wrote back this letter of reconciliation (June 1, 1956):

My Dearest Barbara,

I remember everything you told me the day you left, and believe me I agree whole-heartedly that we can do better. I promised that I would try, and you may be sure I will. Essentially, the things that matter are right — the rest are not beyond repair — right now all my thoughts of you are happy ones — you turned out O.K. and I am supremely satisfied with you the way you are — the storms that come along the way can be weathered, and we will weather them. No human relationship is exactly meant to be a smooth, unruffled affair, and we can't expect to be too different. Essentially, I still say that the important things are in the right places, and we're big enough to straighten out the minor flaws. Who could ask for more?

As ever, my grandmother was unstintingly generous with her daughter, suggesting, for example, that the girls stay at the posh Brown's Hotel in London, a hotel Florence had refused to splurge on for herself on her last visit. But my mother thought it too extravagant.

> I should tell you that we are not staying at Brown's. It was really too high-class for us, so we decided to stay in Russell Square, a little cheaper, good bus connections, and within walking distance of all the shows and the restaurants in Soho. You'd love Brown's because it is beautiful and crispy, but we felt out of our element.

If for no other reason, that summer in Europe was significant to my mother because it forced her to decide her nationality. Florence had given her daughter the gift to choose the country of her passport. She had left for Europe as an American citizen:

> One more bit of news now that it is straightened out. When I got to immigration in Liverpool I was told that I could not travel on your passport and that the letter of permission wasn't worth a hill of beans. Anyway he let me through but said I'd never get any farther on it. I have an appointment for Tuesday — at the American consulate to get my own passport so everything will turn out O.K. Guess I'm an American now for sure.
>
> Love, Barbara

But when my mother was required to recite the American pledge of allegiance and could not easily form the words, she experienced a self-revelation:

> Went down to swear allegiance to George Washington this
> morning — one of the most devastating experiences I
> have ever had. I guess you never know where you stand on
> questions like this until you're face to face with them —
> couldn't be helped though.

Upon her return to Canada, the American citizenship was renounced. If the trip brought on a crisis of national loyalty in my mother, it provoked an emotional crisis in Esther. Halfway through, Esther learned that she had not passed her year. As a result, she would not be welcome back at Whitney Hall. The two friends were devastated. Florence broke the news with characteristic dispatch, in a letter to Salzburg, Austria (delivered July 16, 1956):

> Dearest Barbara,
>
> First of all, congratulations — you made your year, and
> with honours at that. ... But Esther did not!
>
> Barbara, I have been asked by [Esther's parents] to reassure her that they were not upset nor unhappy about her
> results — they feel, and they expressed this thought to us —
> that Esther had a very rough year before she got to the
> U. of T. They are perfectly satisfied that she should go back
> with you for another try, and both Bill and Rose are level-
> headed and intelligent enough to realize that this is far from
> a calamity — it happens to many and they go on to try again
> and succeed — lots worse things can happen in a girl's life,
> as you must both know. Anyway, they feel that the decision
> about next year is Esther's — but they want you to help her

decide to go back to Toronto — that they are perfectly satisfied for her to go back. . . .

All my love, darling, and my most heartfelt congratulations to you — you did well, and I'm proud of you — but I feel that if you had not done so well, I still would have been proud of you and would have loved you, and would have felt that you had gotten enough out of your year at school. The mark you got at the end really didn't matter to me — what mattered was that you got so much education and growth out of every day you spent there last year — how many doors you opened up, and how you enlarged your mind with each opportunity that came along. I couldn't have dreamed up a better attitude or more enthusiastic approach to the University than you had — and I don't know anybody who ever got a bigger lift from a year at school.

Four days later, my mother replied from Munich:

Dear Mom and Dad,

We left Salzburg as soon as we could after receiving your letter. It all seems like a bad dream now that the first shock has worn off. Fortunately we have had a chance to get used to the idea during these last few weeks of not hearing word.

Esther has taken it very well, considering. She is quite upset though and insists she won't go back to start again. The problem of facing old friends, plus the fact that she would have to board out alone is pretty tough to take. We've talked about it quite a bit but I'm afraid no one can say the right thing at times like these. All I want is for her to get back her self-confidence and then I think these other barriers can be gotten over. I suggested that she, Joanie (her friend from Windsor who is coming to U. of T.) and I could perhaps rent an apartment as Esther couldn't get back into residence.

Completely impossible I suppose but something to think about. We've gone over hundreds of ideas today and this was the only one that brought any interest at all.

I hate myself for sending you such depressing letters and only hope you'll try to understand. I hope that in a few days though, things will look different again to us. Needless to say, the fact that I passed could hardly matter less at this point. ...

Love, Barbara

After three more days:

Dear Mom and Dad,

Things have just taken a new direction again, and I thought you'd be glad to hear about it. ... Last night when we came back from the zoo Esther dropped off to sleep from exhaustion and I sat in the lobby for a while and then went to dinner on my own... You know I can't stand to feel my way to a decision, I like to think it out (and talk it out of course) whereas Esther for the past few days has been letting herself get battered back and forth, hoping that the bright day would dawn when everything would be all right again. Well, I decided that as much as she would like to, she can't leave now, nor can she fly home; therefore she must make the best of what is left, for if she's going to mope she might as well go to Liverpool and wait for the boat.

So I got up my strength, went back upstairs and delivered my most thumping pep speech and sure enough it did the trick. We talked and talked and gradually argued her out of all her little worries that have been gnawing away at her for the past two days. Naturally she won't forget about them — but the main thing is that she seems prepared to go back now and not repeat but just take an extra year of courses that she loves anyway. That seems the only way to think of it to me.

So everything seems brighter this morning and we're going to finish the trip in a pile of glory no matter what. . . .

All my love, Barbara

Paradoxically, Esther's bad news worked out well for my mother. The two moved off-campus together. It was through Esther that my mother would soon meet my father, the love of her life. And, outside the walls of Whitney Hall, my mother was freed from the rules of courtship as enacted by the Mistress of Deportment. She could meet her future husband on an equal footing.

Murray Frum, graduate in dentistry

Chapter 4

The Meeting with Murr

MARGARET ATWOOD:

The question I'd like to ask you is would you give up your job for a moment of swept-away passion, Barbara?

BARBARA FRUM:

No, not one moment. But a lifetime of it. . . .

MARILYN FRENCH:

Ah, but a lifetime is never guaranteed. You'd never get that.

THE JOURNAL, *October 1989*
A Women's Issues Panel

THE DAY BEFORE my mother's funeral, our rabbi, Arthur Bielfeld, came by my parents' home to prepare his eulogy. The house was full of mourners, and so that we could have some privacy, my father, brother, and I sequestered ourselves in my parents' bedroom with him.

The rabbi sat in a brown leather sling chair, an object acquired on one of my parents' many trips to Italy. David and my father sat on my parent's Japanese-inspired bed. I sat on the floor, only about four inches lower. As the Rabbi later described the scene: "We were surrounded by Barbara's books, her beads, her pottery, the African artefacts that illuminated her room as clearly as the light flooding in from her garden windows — and Barbara was there; and she was not there."

He said, "Just talk to me about Barbara."

We did.

"A day or two before she died," my father said quietly, "she said to me, you know Murray, in thirty-five years of marriage, we never hurt each other. You never hurt me and I never hurt you." My father paused. "And that was absolutely true," he added, and again to himself, "it was absolutely true."

At her funeral the next day, the Rabbi delivered his eulogy. He was so touched to have learned, he said, that in thirty-five years of marriage, Barbara and Murray *never had a fight*. In the front row of the synagogue, six pairs of eyebrows lifted.

In the limousine on the way to the cemetery, David asked quizzically, "What was that part about you and Mum never having a fight?" There was a moment of quiet and then, not able to help ourselves, everyone in the car burst into laughter. "Remember all the times they shoved us into our snowsuits," David continued, "threw us out into the snow, and slammed the door in our faces so that they could keep on fighting without upsetting us?" We laughed again. Even in that moment, as we were driving to bury her, my mother was so much alive.

Nothing was more vital to my mother than her extraordinary marriage. Whatever else she did in her life, this marriage was her greatest accomplishment, the source of her largest joy. My mother once said, perhaps with a trace of smugness, "Murray and I are the last married couple we know. They'll have to put us in a zoo to study us."

A study of their marriage would have to include their fights, which were many, but almost entirely confined to the early years when my parents, like most newlyweds, sorted out the power-balance between them. As they got older, a peaceful and respect-ful harmony was achieved, and after I reached the age of ten, I can't say I witnessed a single quarrel. (Except those in rental cars in the fields of Europe, when my father behind the steering wheel would demand: "Where are we?" And my mother, holding her map vertically, then horizontally, would plead, "Why? Do you think we're lost?")

Because they argued so little in their later years, they took a nostalgic pleasure in reviewing past disputes. I heard many times about the argument that almost sank their marriage before it started. When my mother declared that she had no desire to main-tain a Kosher home my father was shocked. It had never occurred to him that Jews could do that.

"I'm not saying we can't have a Kosher home," my mother argued, "I'm just saying that if you want one, then *you* can make the special trips to the Kosher butcher, *you* can be responsible for wash-ing two different sets of dishes and cutlery, and *you* can clean the house at Passover."

It was my father's first clue, though not his last, that he was not marrying Betty Crocker.

Another early argument took place on a steaming summer day when my parents had planned a dinner party. Before my father left for his air-conditioned office in the morning, he asked my mother if she might clean the water fountain outside the front door. Arriv-ing home much later, he encountered an uncleaned fountain, a kitchen in disarray, food bubbling over the stove, and, I suppose, children running riot. My mother was in the bathroom, madly putting herself together.

"I thought you were going to clean up the fountain," said my father off-handedly, with provocative detachment. My mother erupted. Half an hour later, when the first guests walked down the path, my parents were still at it.

"Quiet!" said my father who could see them approaching through the window. "Here come our guests."

"I don't care!" bellowed my mother. Overhearing this, the guests hastily retreated. By the time they returned my father had been converted to my mother's point of view.

"If people think I'm a strong, domineering, tough lady and therefore Murray must be a mouse that only goes to show how stereotyped their minds are," my mother once explained to *Home-maker's Magazine*. "He's a strong domineering tough type all on his own. That's the dirty little secret of our life. I guess the real mystery is how two such strong types can get along."

"Murray is very easy to please," her mother-in-law had assured my mother, without irony, before her wedding, "so long as you do everything the way he likes it."

It took my father some time to master the idea that he had married a woman who did not like to make beds (still rebelling against those velvet bedspreads), clean the house, or mop floors. "I may be a slob, but I'm sincere," read a card my mother presented to my father in their first year of marriage. My father's response was to shrug his shoulders, don rubber gloves, and clean up himself. For a man of my father's generation and upbringing, this was a substantial concession.

"We had a very traditional match when we first got married," my mother once explained. "And even now there are certain things one of us does better than the other. When he cooks (which is rare) he does things like pour the chicken fat down the drain. Sometimes I think he does it just to prove to me how hopeless he is in the kitchen. But on the other hand, he has more capacity for detail than I, and he generously exercises it. I think that in most successful marriages, men and women trouble-shoot for each other constantly. It's like having a full-time, live-in agent, confidant, muse and critic — someone who is always working for you. And you do the same for him."

When pushed to explain the success of her marriage, my mother's sincere theory was that it was plain good luck. "Marriage is a lottery," each of my parents would claim, and using this analogy, they had hit the jackpot. My mother once compared marriage to soldering a joint. "The solder either takes or it doesn't. If you have to work at your marriage, it's not a good one."

My parents were never self-congratulatory. "We were blessed with success, wealth, children," my mother told me during one of our endless conversations about love, sex and marriage. "It is easy to be happy when you have all that. Would we have been happy without those things? Who can say?"

Luck was with them from the beginning. For example, they met on a blind date. What are the odds against falling in love with someone casually selected to get you out of your roommate's way? My father's close school chum, Alan Borovoy (today general counsel of the Canadian Civil Liberties Association), wanted to spend an evening alone with Esther in the apartment she and my mother shared at 224 St. George Street. To accomplish this, Borovoy begged his pal Murray to ask Barbara out. He did, and my future parents went off to see a movie: *Solid Gold Cadillac*, with Judy Holliday. Four months later they were engaged. Eight months later they were married.

"My marriage should have been a disaster," my mother would say. "I was so young. I had absolutely no idea of what I was doing. But Murray wanted it so much that I took a chance on him. And he was so right about us. After that I learned, that when Murray wanted something — do it. It's right."

Their wedding took place on my father's twenty-sixth birthday, September 3, 1957, five days short of my mother's twentieth and two years before she was due to graduate. Although shocked in retrospect at how young she was, twenty was the average age for brides in 1957.

When my mother described their courtship, she described my father as a man who knew his mind, who made executive decisions — "a marriage between us would be good" — and had the persuasive skill to carry them out.

The circumstances of their upbringings could hardly have been more different. My father, born in Toronto in 1931, was the only child of Polish-Jewish parents who emigrated to Canada in 1929. My paternal grandparents, Saul and Rebecca Frum, eked out a living from their small, College Street convenience store. My father grew up in the apartment behind and above the store, which for a dozen years was shared with assortments of relatives newly arrived from Poland. As a boy, he slept on the living room couch, because the three bedrooms were taken. When he finally got his own bed, the pillowcases were made from old sugar bags.

Like many of his generation, he understood from childhood that the way out of deprivation was education. At age twelve, he industriously persuaded his parents not to exile him to the subsidized, Yiddish summer camp where poor children were sent to escape polio, but to let him take a job at the St. George Street public library. For twenty-five cents an hour, he disappeared into the stacks and devoured books on history and literature. During the school year, his parents steadfastly refused to let him help them in the store. If there was time for work, they reasoned, there was time for study.

While my mother was sent to college with $1,500 for expenses — the cost of a nice car in 1956 — my father put himself through dental school working at the Christie biscuit plant, and selling Fuller brushes door-to-door. My mother's family vacationed at the Banff Springs Hotel. My father bluffed his way into a position as a waiter there by describing himself (not too inaccurately) as "blond" and "blue-eyed" on the application form, and lying about his skills in "French service". (Until then, he had only known "Yiddish service".)

While my mother won effort awards and graduated from high school with average marks, my father played truant for almost all of his senior year at Harbord Collegiate, preferring to devote his days to an interest in photography, and to a young woman named Betty. In the last weeks before the all-important grade thirteen department exams, he taught himself the entire year's curriculum by late night cramming. In a feat of intellectual wizardry, he scored well enough to win a place in the University of Toronto's Dentistry School, which notoriously limited Jewish students by quota.

Despite my mother's image as a hard-as-nails interviewer, it was my father who was confident and self-assured. "When I first met your mother," my father tells me, "she prefaced each of her remarks with 'I know this will sound stupid'. She was a strange mixture of insecurity and total security. A very interesting mixture. She was always kind of dubious about her own abilities but she also had a real sense of herself, you could never put her down. She was never afraid of being called stupid, because she didn't think she was."

My father, on the other hand, felt so little self-doubt that when a university English professor gave him a failing grade on an essay entitled, 'Was Milton Successful?' my father rejected the professor's harsh remarks. "His criticism is invalid as far as I am concerned," he scribbled on the back of his essay. "I consider it my best work to date!"

My father is a large man, six feet two inches, with an athletic build. But his intimidating figure is softened by gentle green eyes and a sweetness of expression. Although my mother was not inclined to gush that he was handsome, he has always had some quality, not unrelated to good looks, but more connected to his vibrancy, that people find appealing. My girlfriends have always thought him a teddy bear — though I suppose you would have to ask his business acquaintances for an alternative view. My mother was still growing into her own good looks when she accepted her blind date. She had the distinction of becoming more beautiful with age. "Barbara," says my grandmother, "became beautiful after Murray got to her."

My father has always possessed a broad knowledge of many subjects. Most of what he knows, other than dentistry, is self-taught. It amused my father when they were out on dates that my mother asked him questions like: "Who owns the banks?" It impressed him that she didn't pretend to know more than she did. And it impressed my mother that my father could give knowledgeable answers to her questions, no matter how obscure. On one early date, he bowled her over with a minute account of battles and generals in World War II. She later told David: "When I met Murr, I knew I was going to have to run as fast as my chubby little legs could carry me just to keep up."

Her brother Gerry summed up her feelings for him when he said in his memorial speech: "You cannot begin to understand Barbara unless you have a sense of how she felt about her husband. Barbara held no one in awe, but the person who came closest to occupying that position was Murray."

As for my father, legend has it that he decided to marry my mother after their second date. He invited her to a birthday party for the wife of his tennis partner. It hadn't occurred to him to bring a birthday present, but my mother showed up with a chocolate apple which unfolded into neat slices. The cleverness and thoughtfulness of this gesture left a lasting impression.

That may not sound like the clinching argument for a life-long pledge but by the standards of the day, a second date was serious. With young women expecting to marry before the release of the freshman exam schedule, there was enormous pressure to reach quick decisions. The "three date rule", which today provides the cue for young people to start sleeping together, was then a sign that a wedding was in the works.

Although I remember my parents as a romantic couple, from most accounts their courtship was emphatically practical. Esther remembers it this way: "Murray was very persistent. Right off the bat he wanted to give her his frat pin. She said no. Then a couple of weeks later he asked again. She said she'd take it just to keep him quiet. Later, he wanted to give her a school ring. She would come back and say, 'Oh, he really wants me to take this ring.' They went out every Saturday night. He took her to his dental office and showed her the equipment. I remember Barbara saying things like, 'He's nice. He's going to make a good living.'"

But there was more to it than that. There was mutual recognition, and a deep, almost instantaneous bonding. At a party shortly before they were engaged, my father urged my mother to dance with him. My father had been the Harbord Collegiate champion ballroom dancer. (It wasn't his own talent that propelled him but that of his dance partner, the tallest girl in the school, who sweet-talked my vertically unchallenged father into service.)

When my father held out his arm for a waltz, my mother was forced to explain that she couldn't dance.

"You see, it's my right arm," she relayed with as much charm as possible, "it doesn't work."

My father twirled her onto the dance floor and suavely replied: "That's okay. We'll use your left." With that he plunged her into a swoon that lasted thirty-five years.

Perhaps because they were such a good, sensible match, my mother had a difficult time persuading her parents that she was in love. Florence and Harold feared their practical daughter might be making too practical a choice. My mother attempted to put aside their fears.

"Dear Mom and Dad," she wrote shortly after they met Murr, "I am so happy that Murray likes you all so much, because you know, I always hoped it would be that way. We wondered last night too, whether you were still afraid that it was all black and white or whether you too see the affair in Technicolor the way we do. I just had the feeling at that Bar Mitzvah, that the whole world was staring at us, and envying us. That must be the way every couple talks, but who cares. We're right."

When she married Murray, my mother acquired her ultimate best friend. In a profile that appeared in *Chatelaine* in 1972 (when my mother was host of *As It Happens*) Michele Landsberg wrote: "Insiders complain privately that the Frums are a group unto themselves. They don't let their hair down, get drunk or flirt at parties and somehow that sets them at a little distance from the glittering crowd who make each other into famous personalities by publicizing one another's talents."

She *didn't* flirt, and she didn't like flirtatiousness in others. She never took her marriage for granted. No matter how casual the day, she always dressed and made herself up for dinner. When she and my father were at home on the weekend, she cooked an elegant meal and served it on fine china by candlelight. An effort was made, though it was not a labour. It was the joy of her life to make the marriage always seem like an event. She believed in the sacred wholeness of it, and never succumbed to the delusion that it could be elastic.

Despite their exacting careers, my parents spent only a handful of evenings apart. In the early seventies, my father considered expanding his real estate development business into the United States. On the way to the airport for his first business trip to New York, he pondered the innumerable business trips that would accompany any American expansion. Thinking of my mother, he turned his car around, abandoning the trip altogether. "I don't want to live like that," he told himself.

During my own dating years, my mother advised me: "You're not looking for someone without neurosis: you are looking for someone whose neuroses complement yours."

For me, the strength of their marriage was evident when they walked in the door after a three-week voyage together to some place like Yemen, or Florida, where they would have had little to do besides talk to one another. They would enter the house in mid-sentence, as though the conversation that had begun when they climbed into the airport limousine on the way out to the airport was still in full swing. Milan Kundera says that love is an interrogation in which you can never learn enough about your lover. It could be said that my father was my mother's most important interview subject, the one from whom she sought all the answers.

The young reporter, late sixties

Chapter 5

Making Herself Useful

What I don't like is the television view of women from
the womb out, intervening always with the ducts and
glands of the situation: the suggestion that females must
ultimately be captives of their biology, that all our conscious thoughts and actions, our yearnings to make a
mark on the world, will forever be subject to the whims
of our hormones and endocrines.

BARBARA FRUM, *in her television column,*
in Saturday Night, June 1967

BY THE TIME my mother was twenty-six, she was a university
graduate married to a man she adored. She and my father had fulfilled the idle dream of touring Europe for months, shipping a TR3
sports car home as a souvenir. Together with my father, my mother
had designed and built her own home and had two young children.
David was born in June of 1960 and I in January 1963.

"I was happy as a clam," she told Heather Robertson ten years
later. "Nobody can believe it. I was blissfully happy, just completely
enchanted with being a mother...and entertaining friends and
going out to dinner. I had never thought about a job. I was heading

into being a very scientific wife and mother. That's what my mother had done. I read, I studied, I intellectualized what my child was doing. I felt that what I was doing was really worthwhile."

She wasn't a scientific mother, she was an intuitive, loving one. On an audio tape she recorded during baby David's first visit to Niagara Falls (a foreshadowing of the journalist she was to become), a cacophony of voices can be heard. My mother is cooing at David while the rest of her family chats, though not necessarily about the baby. Suddenly, my mother's agitated voice demands: "Everyone be quiet! I just want pure unadulterated baby!" From a journalistic point of view, this was a bad move — David's gurgles were less articulate than they were later to become and this is one of the few recordings that exist of Harold's voice — but there is no doubt that each of us children, from the moment we arrived, was enveloped in love.

The decision to advance from a life devoted entirely to motherhood was unplanned, even reluctant. Strangely, it was not my mother but my father who first thought that Barbara would become a happier person if she had something outside the home to occupy her. My mother was still operating under the rules of the day, as she knew and described them to my high school graduating class in 1981:

> I can tell you, a revolution has happened since the June day when I left school for the last time, when Convocation speakers seemed to address themselves exclusively, and quite unselfconsciously, to the young men in the audience. It was able, ambitious young men the world was waiting for — men of talent to be the future leaders of Canada.
>
> We were to be their wives and their advisers. And of course the mothers of the great men we'd bear and raise to succeed them.

That's why we'd studied English language and literature, modern history, sociology — to be good citizens — aware, involved, able to keep our hands in.

The world was explicitly a place you entered two by two, like the passengers of old Noah's Ark. And though a few ambitious ones eventually went on to get the kinds of jobs bright, articulate young women with B.A.s tended to get in the fifties — we taught school, 'did research', talked of careers 'in publishing' — it occurred to almost none of us that we could make a name for ourselves. Names in our own right.

My father's insistence that my mother try to make a name was echoed by Florence who herself had just discovered a career. The year after Gerry started high school in 1960, my grandmother became a high school English teacher across the Niagara Falls border. She felt that her daughter had a contribution to make to society. My father feared that unless my mother made that contribution, their marriage would suffer.

As he once put it: "When a man gets out of school and starts a profession, he grows along with it. If he gets a helpmate who's stuck away in the house all day, ten years from now, the marriage is in trouble."

And it wasn't only my father and grandmother. The air around her was suddenly thick with imprecations against the shallow comfort of domestic bliss.

In *The Feminine Mystique*, published the year I was born, Betty Friedan warned her readers of "a sense of dissatisfaction" that afflicted "the middle twentieth century housewife" as she "made the beds, shopped for groceries, matched slipcover material, ate peanut-butter sandwiches with her children, chauffeured Cub Scouts and Brownies, lay beside her husband at night."

My mother's friend, the producer and writer Geraldine Sherman, said: "There was this phenomenon working at the time which I call the interesting couple syndrome. There was a real premium placed on being part of an interesting couple. It was old-fashioned in that it was still expected that you would be interesting within the confines of a *couple*, but I suspect a lot of men encouraged their wives to go out into the workforce not because they needed the money, but because they wanted to be part of the interesting couple world. It began to be embarrassing to say I just work at home."

The first cautious step into the professional world was to duplicate, in a professional capacity something my mother was doing anyway: being an uber-mother. With the help of five high school volunteers and the sponsorship of the Ontario Mental Health Society, she developed a program for children from "culturally deprived" homes. She would pick them up in her car, and take them on a tour of the harbour, or to a library, or to an art gallery.

Her efforts gained her some media attention, and my mother went on a speaking tour around Northern Ontario to popularize the concept in other communities. One small town newspaper labeled her a "Mary Poppins" and quoted her as saying: "Many of the children who live in homes crowded with other children, worried parents, and no money, nor books, have never heard a fairy tale, or leafed through a picture book. When we have so much it is hard to visualize children with no opportunity to make these basic discoveries of childhood. ... Some of them cannot communicate because of speech defects, possibly because no one really has time to listen to them when they do talk."

For David and me, here was our first taste of a mother trying to reconcile a career with her maternal duties. We resisted. We were not ready when, on one of our regular visits to Toronto's old Riverdale Zoo, she announced: "I'm just going to make one stop." A dozen strange kids (perhaps fewer, I wasn't counting) suddenly tumbled into our car, pushed us aside, and gobbled up our mother's attention. Her delight in this was no comfort.

She had little sympathy for our complaints. This was the beginning of the bargain my mother would strike with us: in exchange for a more interesting childhood, we would get less of her. Any whining about "why do those other kids have to come with us?" would be met with guilt-inducing lectures about *noblesse oblige.* My mother had decided that it was just as instructive for us to mix with these kids as vice versa.

It is not sour grapes on my part to say that eventually, even my mother would come to disapprove of this Lady Bountiful approach to charity. June Callwood was a director of the Canadian Mental Health Society at that time, and already a renowned journalist. She was destined to become one of my mother's closest friends. She agrees that my mother's well-intentioned program was misguided. "It was that primitive Victorian model of giving charity — the only kind of charity we knew. But Barbara moved on from it, recognizing the flaws."

Charitable activity remained a major part of my mother's life. It evolved from volunteer work, but remained deeply personal. My mother never thought that charity meant writing a cheque for a tax receipt, although she did that too. (More typical was the contribution she made to the Flying Bulgar Klezmer Band at a time when they were having difficulty raising money to finance a CD. The band invited her to come to the dingy Clinton's Bar on Bloor Street West to hear their music. She was charmed and moved to find young people possessing a talent for this antiquated form of Jewish music and became a generous investor. Shortly after her death, her estate received the first royalty cheque of fifty dollars.)

At the time of her work with the Mental Health Society, my mother, with emerging feminist views, came to believe that volunteerism is a trap for women. "The currency today for a job well done is money and [women] are kidding themselves if they believe otherwise," she once said. "Why should women provide free labour? Their husbands don't respect them for doing it."

Notwithstanding such emancipated statements, my mother still stressed what was warm and domestic. In a profile written in 1966, during her tour to promote her program, a reporter from the *Sault Saint Marie Star* observed that besides her volunteer work, "Barbara finds time to collect paintings, knit sweaters for her children, make the majority of her own clothing and pursue the study of archaeology."

Only two years before she was to become co-host of a current affairs show, my mother still was not thinking of a full-fledged career. "She never got up one morning and said, I'm going to be a journalist," according to my father. "It was not a thought-through process. Each project led to the next. The mental health project led to being interviewed by Lorraine Thompson on *Trans Canada Matinee*, which led to them asking her if she would come back and do a series over the summer on where-to-take-kids-for-amusement. That led to other freelance radio assignments. And that led to freelance writing. There was never a decision that, okay, now I'm in the workforce. It was an evolution."

My mother herself wrote, "I haven't plotted my life like Napoleon's campaigns. Anyway, look what happened to Napoleon."

Much of her progress was good luck, for instance, her fortuitous encounter with June Callwood. As June remembers it: "Mrs. Frum, the dentist's wife, was a name that stuck with me [from the Mental Health Society project.] One day I was in a gallery, maybe it was Dorothy Cameron's, and a woman came to me from across the room and said, 'I'm Barbara Frum.' After chatting just a little bit she said, 'you and your husband must come to our house for dinner.' I found everything about her so overwhelming. She was younger than I by fifteen years. She must have been twenty-nine years old at that point. And her composure: the sense that it was perfectly appropriate to say, 'how do you do and come to dinner' to someone you've never seen before. And I, who am very shy about going to small gatherings of strangers — I hate that intensely — I said, 'We'd love to.'

"My impression was that she was an odd card, not a rule player. That endeared me to her. She was someone with enterprise and gusto: a kind of enthusiasm for life that was very contagious. I could see she was way brighter than I was and I was flattered that she thought there was something I could give her."

June became a mentor. When my mother discovered that a charity was collecting money to find a cure for tuberculosis, long after the cure had already been found, it was June who encouraged her to sell the story to the *Toronto Star*.

"My first blissful beginning memories are about calling the *Toronto Star* and asking to see the already legendary Ralph Allen," my mother told writer Susan Crean. "This was absurd, bloody absurd. What was more absurd was that he saw me. I must have been shaking. A person who is putting out a daily newspaper has got a lot of things to do besides talk to someone off the street who claims to have a story. I had it all typed, though, and left it with him. He said he'd get back to me, which he did, and asked me to come in again, which I could hardly believe."

Allen battered my mother, demanding at least four rewrites of the story. When she was finished, he ran it on the front page. It was a glittering launch for a print career. "I was quite excited with myself," said my mother, "and became infatuated with this notion you could know something other people didn't and get it printed in the newspaper."

Soon there was another important encounter. At a party at June's house in 1966, my mother was introduced to Peter Gzowski, then entertainment editor of the *Toronto Star*. These two legends of radio first met each other as print people. Gzowski offered her a column on the subject of radio in the TV age, which she accepted. From that, she became TV columnist for *Saturday Night* in 1967.

Gzowski does not remember my mother as a great writer. "Barbara was never a print journalist," he says. "Barbara was a broadcast genius, waiting to find broadcasting."

Robert Fulford, who was a daily columnist at the *Toronto Star* in 1967, disagrees. "Barbara made her radio column interesting but it was an entry level thing to do. It was a great kind of column that you could take anywhere. I think she could have been a terrific writer if she had wanted to. Most writers start off sounding like everyone else. Many years go by and they still sound like everyone else. But Barbara never sounded like anyone else. She had an ear. She could think. She had a lot of energy. All that adds up to a great writer."

Peter Newman, who published a number of my mother's freelance articles after he became editor of *Maclean's* in 1971, said that, "What impressed me was not her writing style, because she never was a stylist, but her research, which was indomitable. She really *went* at a subject...she felt she had to write the truth — not just get the facts, but get the truth, which often is slightly different and a lot harder."

It would be wrong of me and my mother would disapprove if I portrayed her entry into journalism as a steep and steady rise. In a scrapbook where she kept clippings and mementoes of her career it is the rejection notices — a dozen of them — which are prominently displayed on the front pages.

Some of them were harsh and insulting, like the one from the women's editor of the *Toronto Telegram*, dated June 23, 1965:

Dear Mrs. Frum,

I apologize for holding this manuscript for such a long time. ... We decided not to buy it, feeling that it was too one-sided. I would suggest, if you are still interested in putting forward this view, that you reduce it to Letter to the Editor size.

Others were encouraging. One from Harry Bruce at *Saturday Night* in April 1965 says:

I found your piece on lawyers' discrimination against women [jurors] quite interesting and think that if you want to gamble the time on developing it some more you might have a good, short, sharp piece that would be worth $75 to us. I say gamble because I'm afraid I can't guarantee anything till I see a new version of the piece.

While someone else might have burned these letters, my mother carefully preserved them. In her *Journal* years, she could not give a speech to a group of students without telling them that "when I started out, I faced a lot of rejection."

I suspect it was that same impulse that made her ask if she could keep an especially humiliating photograph of me from the Regina *Leader-Post*. Some months after I wrote a guide to Canadian universities, I delivered a talk at the University of Regina on "Why this university is Canada's worst." Oddly, despite such an inviting title, only five, perhaps six, students showed up. (Well, there were more, but that's what it felt like.) Inexperience prevented me from suggesting that we just go to the campus pub and discuss the matter over beer. Instead, I carried on stolidly in the largest auditorium on campus. A mischievous photographer for the *Leader-Post* snapped me from behind the stage: intensely addressing an empty hall. The picture ran half a page.

When I got home I showed the newspaper to my mother.

"Oh I *love* it!" she said in the slow, drawling way she did when she thought something really funny. "Trust me Linda, you'll find this funny some day too."

She had swelled my courage and I conceded, "It's funny even now."

Even in her very first articles, my mother displayed a remarkable gift for asking questions. In Toronto for a meeting with Canadian franchise holders, the famous Colonel Sanders told her that the Canadian franchisees were "falling down on the baked beans, the 'slaw and the macaroni salad."

"Are you serving chicken to the boys?" she asked.

"No, honey," she reported him as saying. "When we get together Ah like to serve them something a little different for a treat, maybe some lobster newburg or prime ribs of beef."

This ability soon got her into trouble. Janet Malcolm says all journalism is seduction and betrayal. My mother denied that she tried seduction. "I don't use sex," she would say of her interviewing technique. Perhaps because she seemed unseductive, she was trusted more, and her subjects were indiscreet. A *Maclean's* article she wrote in 1971 was entitled, "Thanks Darling, for making me what I am today." It was a profile of eight Canadian wives, "big winners in the marriage sweepstakes . . . who have achieved status through the reputations and power of their husbands." Each woman speaks in the first person. Responses to my mother's questions are strung together, the questions cut out. Although this gave the appearance of utter objectivity, my mother's purpose — to portray the difficulty of living in the shadow of a powerful man — is not hard to detect. And the wives, most of them obviously unhappy, poured out their feelings to her.

Later, my mother told Michele Landsberg in *Chatelaine*: "I really had to search my soul about that one. When good friends attacked me for writing it, I had to consider whether I had done the right thing. I came to the conclusion that, since those women agreed freely to speak to me, and were presented strictly in their own words, well, it must have been that they needed or wanted to talk. I certainly didn't feel that I was judging them in any way; on the contrary, I assumed that women readers would feel the same empathy, the same urge to be good to your sisters because this is what we are all struggling with, that is what I felt."

The scars showed most on Mrs. Pierre Berton, whom my mother introduced by saying, "When she married Pierre she was an established reporter on a Vancouver newspaper, the kind of reporter, remembers an editor, that 'when you sent Janet the competition had to send five.'" She then quoted Janet Berton:

> Our family life revolves around Pierre. I think it has to. I think that, Women's Lib notwithstanding, you really can't have two prima donnas in one family and somebody's got to give in. ... I think it would be dynamite to try to be competent in the same field as Pierre. Especially Pierre. ... The only problem I find having him so productive is that he makes all the rest of us look like absolute slobs. I do all his proofreading. And I have done a lot — well, a little bit — of his research. Pierre told me the other day that nobody could proofread like me, and that was kind of nice, and it made it all worthwhile, the fact that I'd been up until 3:30 the night before proofreading.
>
> I don't resent spending my time picking up socks ordinarily. Well, sometimes, when he complains about where his shoe polish is, which is what we had a little scene about the other day.

There was also Rompin' Ronnie Hawkins's wife, who said,

> When we first got married he'd come home with lipstick on his shirt or on his neck, or whatever. On his ear. And, um, I'd

see that and I wouldn't say anything. And he'd say next day, 'Oh gee, I've got lipstick on my shirt.' And I'd say, 'Yes. Just like you had the last time.' But it's all right because as long as he comes home when he's supposed to come home, or even if he comes home later, it's all right because I know how he is with his children and with me.

My mother wasn't patient with women like that.

I remember as a teenager going with her to the Bertons' fabled, annual Kleinburg picnic. Despite their graciousness (which began with the invitation) I detected frostiness in the air. When I commented on it to my mother, she explained, "I once published something about Janet and her daughters have never forgiven me." I perceived regret and remorse as she added defensively: "All I did was write down what she said!"

It was always dangerous to be interviewed by Barbara Frum.

The Way It Is, *1971*

Chapter 6

Trials, Errors

BARBARA FRUM:

Are you aware that a lot of women are in love with you?

BILL COSBY:

Sure. But...it's not the kind of thing when housewives throw their hotel keys up on the stage à la Frank Sinatra. I think most people look at me like a groovy neighbour. Other women — well anything they see on the screen — a lot of chicks dig Mickey Mouse 'cause he's on the screen. You know, women are weird.

THE DAY IT IS, *March 1969*

IN 1969, CBC TV PUBLIC AFFAIRS was ruled by Ross McLean. My mother met him when she interviewed him for an article she was writing about public versus private broadcasting.

McLean had already heard about my mother from colleagues who were encouraging him to consider her for a position on air. He was unimpressed by their stories, imagining my mother to be an unpleasant, "pushy, dentist's wife." As he told the *Toronto Star*: "People had been urging her on me. Everybody, it seemed to me, on every occasion they could think of. This kind of campaign, it almost seemed to be a lobby. I got this sense of some awful aggressive lady. I wasn't at all persuaded that she was what I needed."

After their first meeting, McLean had "a curious reverse response". When she didn't try to angle him for a job, he wanted to give her one.

Robert Fulford says that McLean was "a natural television producer," who possessed an intuitive understanding of the medium. He knew before most that television needed to be more dynamic than simply radio with pictures. Perhaps that is why McLean favoured the shock-appeal and, of course, sex-appeal of women television hosts, or, in the vernacular of the times, "public affairs girls". At a time when common gospel dictated that: "news is handed down from God and God sounds like a man," McLean showed a unique interest in female talent. Not to suggest that McLean was the decade's most enlightened feminist. Praising his new public affairs girl to the *Toronto Star* in 1968, McLean said of my mother: "She's not one of these brass-bound bitches struggling, clawing, her way up the ladder whom we see so much of around here." Rather, she possessed "a kind of casualness about a career that is very appealing."

What McLean took to be an "appealing casualness" was, I suspect, a misreading of a more subliminal message. Many years later, and in another context, my mother said: "You know Linda, there is only one good reason to have money and that is so you can say: 'Fuck you, I don't need you,' to anybody. (During the *As It Happens* years she used at least one expletive per sentence. But this conversation occurred long after she had carefully suppressed that habit, which is why I remember her saying "fuck you" so clearly.)

The Way It Is was created in 1968 to replace the hugely successful but scandalous *This Hour has Seven Days* as the CBC's leading current affairs program. *The Way It Is* had no single host, but many rotating contributors which put McLean in possession of the producer's fabled commodity: the means to fasten attention on a new face and "make her a star." Typically he preferred models and blond bombshells. One of his discoveries was the gorgeous Joyce Davidson. Another blond star, Jean Templeton, became his wife.

Robert Fulford says, "Ross had two or three stars before Barbara. But they were definitely softer. They were there to please. Barbara was a new era."

My mother, who confessed to the *Toronto Star* in a 1968 interview that she was no Zsa Zsa Gabor, was mystified by McLean's sudden change in taste.

"I too have been brainwashed to think glamour is a necessary component of television. Like with Joyce Davidson — well I used to watch her on *Tabloid* just to watch her face! Ross McLean sure didn't pick me for glamour. Maybe he's changed his image of what a woman should be like. Or maybe he has others in mind for glamour. Maybe they're still in his card file..."

My mother never had illusions about her appearance. She made an effort to be fashionable, with a short, 1960s, mop-top hairdo, leather mini-dresses, and pastel make-up. Such fashion items detracted terribly from her strengths, but had the positive effect of forcing the audience to pay attention.

Perhaps this was the secret behind McLean's interest in her. Because she did not look like a siren, she made viewers accustomed to them ask: What is *she* doing there? And the answer would be: listen.

Another motive may have been an unpleasant analysis of how female hosts could turn off female viewers. McLean told one television columnist: "I think that deeply submerged in the woman viewer is some degree of envy and hostility to other women. Although she may be doing as good — or better — a job as her male counterpart, the woman performer is criticized by other women for her hairdo, posture, and voice."

An anonymous TV executive says in the same column: "The average woman spends her time in casual clothes, struggling with her kids and housework. How do you think she feels when she turns on the TV set and there in front of her is a poised, perfectly groomed woman, knowledgeably discussing Canada's role in NATO or the latest hassle between Quebec and Ottawa. I'll tell you — she doesn't like it at all. It makes her feel inadequate. She doesn't want to watch, nor does she want her husband to watch."

McLean and his cohorts probably believed that my mother would not be a threat to this Canadian housewife. Unfortunately, her male colleagues were less benign. Robert Fulford remembers, "Barbara told me a story that even after she had been with CBC TV for three years, there was a meeting to plan the holidays of the personnel, and it was said, 'Well, we've got to have *him* here,' — and this is how the sentence ended: 'or we'll have Barbara here reading the news.' And it was like they might have said, 'We'll have Rosie-the-clown here reading the news.' And her attitude was, well, what would be so crazy about that? Whether she was thinking that as a woman, or as Barbara, I'm not quite sure."

The insult stung the more acutely because my mother's skills as a journalist were apparent by then. Though she had some way to go she was already performing as well as the males on the program, who included Patrick Watson, Ken Lefolii, Warren Davis, and Moses Znaimer.

She made plenty of mistakes. In June 1969, she interviewed Jacqueline Susann, (who was promoting her novel, *The Love Machine*). My mother made the novice's slip of approaching the interview as a debate rather than an interrogation. She thought this interview the worst of her career, and when Susann died a few years later of breast cancer, my mother felt sick about it. Here is an excerpt:

FRUM:

> I'm wondering if books for you isn't just sort of the thing you can do.

SUSANN:

Sure it's my thing. And I think I do it well. And I think I'm a good writer.

FRUM:

I've got a lot of respect for good art I guess.

SUSANN:

Well so have I. My father was a portrait painter. What did your Daddy do?

FRUM:

Why?

SUSANN:

Well because you've got such a hang-up about wanting art. My father has portraits in the Academy of Fine Arts, he's painted governors, he's painted supreme court justices. ...

FRUM:

So you think all the art is done in your family you mean.

SUSANN:

No I think it goes on. But I am not hung up to think: Am I doing art? You seem ... what did your father do that makes you so hung up that you must get up in the middle of the night and say: Is it art?

FRUM:

You tell me to go to a shrink. That's a shrink question: What did your father do? I don't think it's relevant. You think it's relevant.

SUSANN:

Are you ashamed of what your father did?

FRUM:

No.

SUSANN:

What did he do?

FRUM:

It's irrelevant to me for this discussion.

SUSANN:

Now I'm curious.

FRUM:

Yeah, good. What did you think of your husband's talents in making [the film] *Valley of the Dolls*? And I assume in this book.

SUSANN:

Well I think my husband is one of the most brilliant men in the world.

FRUM:

No, I'm talking about his promotional skills which I understand played an enormous part in the success of *Valley of the Dolls*.

SUSANN:

Oh, I think he's brilliant.

FRUM:

Do you discount the value of that in the success of *Valley of the Dolls*?

SUSANN:

No of course not. Alone I could be nothing.

FRUM:

You know, I suppose, I've heard you interviewed on American radio and I've always had this feeling of the two of you sitting down and planning...

SUSANN:

No, we don't plan. When we sit down we neck.

FRUM:

Aw, right out of one of your books eh?

SUSANN:

No, not out of my books. They don't just sit down and neck.

FRUM:

No?

SUSANN:

They do other things.

FRUM:

Like what?

SUSANN:

Well, you read them some time, you might find out.

Susann got her revenge by complaining about my mother to a reporter from the *Globe and Mail*: "Such a primitive set. The lighting — impossible. What was the interviewer trying to do? Such a baby. I could have ground her to hamburger — but I'm here only once — poor thing she has to go on with the show every day."

Better than this, the interview made a lasting impression on my mother. Even in the last weeks of life, when we spoke about the harsh treatment of her by a *Globe* reviewer, she tried to diffuse my anger by explaining: "That's how it works. Younger journalists make their reputation by feeding on the old and the established. Young people always pull themselves up by pulling down those ahead of them. How can I blame them?" she said, conjuring up Susann, "I did it too."

Though she was still learning where to draw some lines, her trademark calm and poise were well developed. In an interview with the wife of the Black Panther leader, Eldridge Cleaver, the subject didn't like a question, held a newspaper to her face and pretended to read it. She insisted that six Black Panther bodyguards surround her. Mrs. Cleaver would answer questions in a manner few interviewees ever dare to do. When my mother asked: "Tell me about your own personal style," she replied: "No." My mother remained cool.

By the end of her first season on television, her talent was noticed by the *Toronto Star*'s television critic, Patrick Scott, who deemed her the best new interviewer of 1968. (For the worst, he selected twenty-six-year-old Moses Znaimer, another Ross McLean protégé. And the show itself, he deemed to be the year's worst public affairs series.)

Interestingly, to lend credibility to McLean's theories, it was a female critic, Joan Irwin, of the *Montreal Star*, who was frequently on the attack, mocking my mother's competence, and persistently misspelling her name. A typical Irwin review: "The second last 'The Way It Is' came on like an adolescent last night. . . . The collection of citizens assembled in the studio tried over and over again (at least some of them did) to explain to interviewer Barbara Frumm that obscenity isn't a synonym for sex. They failed completely to get through because the lady (and presumably her superiors on the program) had already decided that the two words are synonymous. . . . This was by a long shot the worst *Way It Is* I've ever seen though I missed last week's effort which I'm told by all who saw it was an excruciatingly simplistic discussion of news gathering."

For its final installment, *The Way It Is* broadcast a panel discussion with its seven hosts. The object was to review the highlights and flaws of the program's two seasons. (I reviewed many tapes of this program: this one was *truly* excruciating.) It is impossible not to read significance into my mother's placement on the panel: seated at the end of the semi-circle, she is just barely squeezed into the frame, the only one shot in profile. Each of the six men has enough elbow room to be shot head-on. Three of the seven, Patrick Watson, Moses Znaimer, and my mother, would become giants of television. Knowing this, it is both funny and frustrating to see that my mother scarcely gets in a word, is interrupted whenever she does speak, and is never called upon for an opinion.

Any woman in that position must learn to be aggressive. My mother was feeling her way between the gentility expected of women, and the aggressiveness needed to be taken seriously.

Part of the hostility of the group is understandable. Only she and Warren Davis had been asked back by McLean to host his new nightly supper-hour current affairs program, *The Day it Is*.

Soon after the new show began, the FLQ initiated the October Crisis of 1970 by kidnapping the British trade commissioner, James Cross, and murdering Quebec's deputy premier, Pierre Laporte. At 4:00 a.m., on October 16, Pierre Trudeau invoked the War Measures Act. The day before, according to Knowlton Nash's *Microphone Wars*, the CBC president, George Davidson, received a phone call in the presence of Nash (then a CBC vice president) from the communications minister, Gérard Pelletier, "to urge that the CBC avoid 'inflammation' of the crisis in its coverage and commentaries."

This official dictum was impressed upon every program and every host. My mother, who was shocked and disgusted by the government's action, thought this a grotesque abuse of power. On the night the Act was invoked, she and her closest friends (many of them in the media) held a wake to mourn what they believed to be a betrayal of civil liberties. When she heard the demand for self-censorship, she promised her superiors that the content and style of her interviews would be altered in no way to suit the agenda of the Prime Minister.

When my mother arrived at the studio to conduct her first War Measures interview, she was told that another reporter would be filling in. She walked out of the studio in outrage. Three months later the CBC made its displeasure perfectly clear by demoting her from hostess to story editor on a revamped *Day It Is*, retitled *Weekday*. The executive producer of *Weekday*, Don Cameron, gave the *Toronto Star* this brutal explanation of his actions: "My immediate concern is *Weekday*'s flaccid midsection, 'Weekday Journal', which has degenerated into 'idle chit-chat' presided over by its hostess, Barbara Frum." According to the *Star* report, "[Cameron] wants to move 'Weekday Journal' away from its nightly (and usually superficial) examinations of parochial 'social problems' and into the much broader area of theater, music and general arts reviews. As the first, imminent step in this direction, Mrs. Frum will be demoted from hostess to reporter, and those meandering seances will be replaced with a more disciplined and more formal magazine format."

Humiliated, my mother quit. Her resignation made the front page of both the Toronto *Telegram* and the *Star*.

She told the *Star*: "Those in charge have given me the impression that they don't value my services. They've changed the job. I was free to stay. I think it's reasonable to assume that there was a desire to limit my on-camera appearances. Not by the executive producer, but by the higher-ups at CBC. ... I was going to quit a month ago but I didn't want anyone to say that I was hot or angry or not prepared to take a new thing."

Her version of these events can be read in her 1976 book, *As It Happened*:

> I quit [TV] when yet another managerial shake-up and lingering timidity following the War Measures Crisis combined to demand QUIET. When my new bosses interpreted that demand to mean 'friendlier' interviews from me personally, I decided to return to freelance writing. For someone who thinks of interviewing as a game full of surprises, it sounded a little too managed for my taste.

My mother's first foray into television ended in failure. Her second, *The Journal*, was a huge success. What changed? Was it my mother? Possibly. Her early interviews did sometimes ramble. But the CBC changed too. The CBC of the sixties still had trouble making room for an intelligent woman, especially one who did not hold the ruling parties of Canada in reverence, as did most of the corporation's executives and senior producers. The audience also changed. The taste for my mother's kind of interviewing grew and grew.

With Harry Brown and Mark Starowicz, 1973

Chapter 7

As It Happens Nightly

SANDRA GOOD:

> You're a very, very bad reporter... You don't have any finesse.
> Now put me onto somebody else.

BARBARA FRUM:

> I'm it, Miss Good. I'm it, I'm afraid.

SANDRA GOOD:

> Are you a man or a woman?

BARBARA FRUM:

> I'm a man.

SANDRA GOOD:

> Are you a man? You are a woman.

BARBARA FRUM:

> Well then, why did you ask?

AS IT HAPPENS, *September 1975*
Interview with room-mate of Lynette Fromme,
the woman who attempted to assassinate President Ford

M<small>Y MOTHER</small> would say that everyone has an interesting story,
it is only a question of getting it out. Her career as an extractor
flowered when she entered the CBC Radio building. In retrospect,
it can be seen that she had the good fortune to be jettisoned from

television at the precise moment when radio temporarily surpassed it in importance.

"The very week I left that television job," my mother wrote in the introduction to her book *As It Happened*, "I was advised to sit tight and wait for the fall radio season. ... The show I was invited to host was deliberately designed to break all the old, safe CBC rules. The orders were: provide an iconoclastic, zippy, nightly information package. Speak to everybody, not just to the few who genuflect to the sound of a mid-Atlantic accent. I've been on the dialing end of a telephone ever since."

CBC Radio had good reasons to break the old rules. By the end of the sixties, listenership had sunk so low that there was serious talk of abolishing the radio network. Knowlton Nash has called this period the "great CBC Radio turn-off" and wrote that: "With the arrival of TV, radio listening had collapsed, and CBC Radio got few headlines, minimum attention from politicians, except for its morning news and commentary, and only passing glances from most senior CBC management."

A study was commissioned — the Ward-Meggs Report — to propose a way to resuscitate CBC Radio, once a national lifeline. To compete with television, radio needed to become less staid and ponderous. It needed, in what became its motto, to be "revolutionized". To accomplish this, two "zippy" new programs were created — *As It Happens* on Monday nights, and Peter Gzowski's *Radio Free Friday*. These programs were such a success that eventually they were merged. The result, heard five nights a week, kept the name *As It Happens*. Gzowski went on to become host of CBC Radio's next hit, *This Country in the Morning*.

The so-called radio revolution was made possible in part by television's own stagnation. Twenty years after its inception, television was bumping against the limits of its cumbersome, studio-based technology. As Val Clery, the original producer of *As It*

Happens realized, radio could take listeners to places that television — in that era before satellites and portable videocams — could not. Radio had at its disposal what remains the world's most brilliantly adaptable communications tool: the telephone.

Although there were already many radio phone-in shows, the idea of having people in the studio initiate the calls, and use the telephone to go *outside* the studio, was ground-breaking. *As It Happens* pioneered a new form of journalism — immediate and irreverent — and used it to discover a new radio audience.

The radio revolution "kind of crept up on people," says Peter Gzowski. "There wasn't the fooferah that there later was with *The Journal. This Country in the Morning* and *As It Happens* became the two daily signposts. We didn't know the degree to which we changed radio until we got this huge response from people."

The non-conformist culture of radio appealed to my mother much more than the culture of television, where pandering to government had seemed to be a self-imposed mandate. Radio was for "radicals" and my mother, who, in never-ending protest against Trudeau's War Measures Act, had become an active member of the Canadian Civil Liberties Association (a unique exception to her rule of non-affiliation), was one of them at that time.

Margaret Lyons, the former vice president of English CBC Radio, and my mother's boss for the ten years she worked in the radio building, invoked CBC Radio's contempt for the TV network to explain my mother's appeal to her: "Anybody who had been trashed by television was perfect for us."

"We were all in our twenties when we started *As It Happens*," says Max Allen. "Today, the gang of kids go to television — anybody with any sense wants to work at City TV." But in 1973, it was to CBC Radio, that chic young journalists gravitated. (Ivan Fecan, Pamela Wallin, Judy Stoffman, and Erna Paris all became story producers at *As It Happens*.) CBC Radio was hip but not prestigious.

"When I went from TV to radio, people thought I was nuts," remarked my mother, not adding that she didn't have much choice.

Philip Forsythe, the original host of *As It Happens*, had gone by the time my mother was hired, joining artist William Ronald and CBC announcers Cy Strange and Harry Brown. At first she and Strange worked as a team, alternating with Ronald and Brown. It soon became clear that my mother had an intuitive feel for the off-beat yet penetrating interviews the show would become famous for. By some magic, her personality and that of *As It Happens* began to blend together.

William Ronald, whom Peter Gzowski describes as "colourful but bombastic", was replaced so that my mother could work five nights a week. "Bill and Barbara were alternating nights, and Barbara just got better," explains Gzowski. Later, nightly hosting duties were assigned evenly to my mother and Harry Brown; so evenly, in fact, that they were expected to do interviews together: two hosts on one guest.

Was this doubling-up done because my mother was still considered a broadcast novice or because she was a woman?

I have been cautioned by a number of my mother's colleagues — both male and female — not to essay an excessively feminist analysis of my mother's career at *As It Happens*. For one thing, my mother was never inclined to think of herself as a feminist heroine. To do that, she would have had to play the victim triumphing over unreasonable obstacles, and even if she was, my mother was constitutionally incapable of thinking like that. Once, asked if she thought that she would have been host of *As It Happens* without a concurrent women's movement, she answered, "Of course." Who knows if she was right?

"She did not go out there and say: I'm going to do this for womankind," Robert Fulford said about her struggle to become a solo host on *As It Happens*. "She was doing it for her own freedom, her own enjoyment, and her own ability to do something well."

It is nonetheless surprising to recall that at the time my mother joined *As It Happens* in 1971, the sound of a woman's voice on radio discussing anything except housework or children was a curiosity. (Kate Aitken and Claire Wallace, Canada's most successful female broadcasters of the forties and fifties, hosted shows whose topics were limited to recipes, fashion, and travel.)

And although CBC Radio was more progressive than perhaps any other broadcaster, there was reluctance to let a woman out on such a limb. "A lot of men used to joke that CBC Radio was a matriarchy," says Geraldine Sherman. "[In the seventies] it was dominated by women, but that was certainly not true on the air. There were no women news readers, and no women current affairs hosts."

"She was a first," says Heather Robertson of my mother. "The first woman broadcasting host. And there was a sense of people waiting for her to fall on her face. It was like a dog walking on its hind legs. But she hung in. And her radio style developed because of that awareness that the knives were out."

The radio style Robertson alludes to was jarring for many listeners. The most frequently used adjective to describe my mother in those days was "aggressive" by which "unfeminine" was insinuated. But my mother, who, though working hard, was still very much a devoted wife and mother, prided herself on not using feminine charm to get ahead. She understood the trap of sex appeal. In the short term it may seduce both audience and guests, but it leads to a frivolous reputation.

"There used to be only two types of women who could make it in broadcasting," said my mother shortly after she joined *As It Happens*. "One type was gracious and womanly. She had a rich, creamy, mellifluous voice. The other woman was a dolly-person — impish, cute, and maybe a little flipped out. That was it."

My mother created a new type, and it was her new type that inspired young women to enter journalism. I think she thought of the profession as gender-neutral and that interviewing had nothing to do with sex, in either sense of the word. You did your research and your reading and dealt with whatever your guest was saying. To do this was still thought of as manly, but my mother knew that it was neither masculine nor feminine, it was just doing the job.

In her graduation address to my high school class some ten years later, she urged young women to embrace this idea. "I hope you will decide to express characteristics in yourselves that have long, frankly, frightened women who considered them the exclusive province of men," she said. "Qualities like ambition, single-mindedness, frankness, competitiveness, impatience with stupidity, and that easy self-esteem and confidence strong men have."

When Mark Starowicz became the executive producer of *As It Happens* in January 1973, he was unprepared for my mother's self-confidence. Starowicz had been Montreal bureau chief for the *Toronto Star* and a producer on *Radio Free Friday*. Although he was — sometimes recklessly — involved in the radical left politics of his day, there were some kinds of radicalism he still had not encountered. An amicable and productive twenty-year partnership had a very rocky start.

"My first memory of Barbara Frum was her insistence on doing the interviews by herself. Harry wanted to divide the interviews and Barbara didn't. Harry could do other interviews but she didn't want to share hers. And really, that makes total sense. The two-on-one interview doesn't exist anywhere else in journalism. But did I know that at the time? No. I didn't know what I was doing. I tied myself to any mast that came along. I was looking for a peaceful road that would make everybody happy."

Starowicz insisted that my mother and Harry Brown share interviews. "We hit it off as wrong as any two people could hit anything off," says Starowicz. "It poisoned the air for the first couple of months. I resented anybody, who, from my point of view, was putting a huge demand on the agenda. I just got this job and all of a sudden somebody is saying, I want to do this and I don't want to do that."

Of course to others, especially to Harry Brown and Mark Starowicz, my mother would seem pushy and demanding. She was unafraid, and they weren't used to that in a young woman. She stood up for herself. She knew that she was talented and would not be kept down. A clash became inevitable.

Mark Starowicz remembers: "I was not enjoying myself and Barbara was really unhappy. Things had been strained to the point where either a separation would occur, or, well...things were just not working out. I don't know who instigated it — I think it was Barbara — but we agreed to meet one weekend at what looked like a Fran's. I remember there were two plates of limp fries with brown gravy on them which neither of us touched. We must have been the scandal of the restaurant. We were yelling at each other. Barbara was quite anguished at that point.

"It was a Polish conversation. I guess we both got it out of our systems because after that we became the greatest pals. I don't remember the details, all I know is that the Starowicz-Frum alliance was made in that place.

"After that, people saw an entente between us. We started to tell each other our troubles. Mine was: I was terrified. Suddenly I had a nightly show, and despite what anyone tells you, you do not get a surge of power. You get a surge of utter, appalling horror. Your mind, if you have the slightest imagination, imagines all the things that could go wrong. I wasn't much better than a kid and everyone else was much younger."

In fact, my thirty-four-year-old mother was the old lady on the set. (For those inclined to believe in fate, it is interesting to note that she and Starowicz share a birthday — September 8 — six years apart.)

The entente was probably helped by this memo (July 26, 1973):

> Recognizing that each has certain specialties, or facility with certain kinds of interviews, we will assign one or the other to do a specific story in pre-tape by themselves. In practice, this will mean two or three stories a day each. Barbara is particularly strong on personality pieces, "psychological" interviews etc. Harry is often strongest on Canadian pieces and some international interviews.

(Note that as late as 1973 the opposite was inconceivable — that a woman might be strong on politics, and a man on personalities.)

Harry Brown and my mother were never a good match. They were always civil to each other but as a child, without understanding why, I recall Brown keeping a wary distance from her. I know that my mother's desire to do her own interviews had very little to do with Brown and much with her own ambitions and sense of craft. It was not that she wanted to hear more of her own voice: she thought the less said by interviewers, the better.

"She may have been the person who discovered that the most powerful thing you can do in an interview is nothing at all, but sit there," explains Max Allen. "And on the phone that's devastatingly effective. She would ask a question, the person would give a terrible answer and she would very often just sit there and wait them out. People with a phone in their hands — and nobody's making any noise — are driven to talk. She could do this better than any other human being I've seen. When we packaged the program, we'd just edit all those long silences out of there. And it looked like she just asked the question and people came up with all of these wonderful answers. You didn't know that she had brow-beaten them by not speaking. She also tended to do this live, which was harder on the audience. The nice thing about being able to edit is that all that horror, which is about 60 percent of interviews, disappears. It was her best trick."

When I first took on some journalistic projects of my own, my mother said one day, "Would you like me to share with you my secrets of interviewing? So many people ask me, but I never tell them. But if you want me to, I'll tell you."

This was thrilling. I remember thinking a full day could be scheduled and that a dozen empty notebooks would be needed to transcribe the sacred commandments. Instead she quickly said: "Use as few words as possible to ask your questions and then get out of the way."

"That's okay, Mum," I said, not yet ready for the flood of wisdom. "We don't have to go over this now. Let's schedule a time to do this properly."

"But I'm finished. That's it."

"What do you mean, 'That's it'?"

"That's it. Never become too entranced with your own voice. Don't forget that the whole point is to hear as little of you and as much of the other guy as possible. Do that and you'll do a good job."

Anyone who has ever done an interview knows it is not that simple. But I don't think my mother was being stingy; the rest of her interviewer's skill was inborn.

Once, on a book tour, an admiring journalist from the *Montreal Star* treated her like the journalistic equivalent of the Amazing Kreskin. He asked her to interview him spontaneously though she had never met him before. As the journalist explained: "Immediately she said: 'That's a rather old-fashioned watch chain you've got hanging from your buttonhole. Is there a watch attached to it in your top pocket?' And I found myself talking away about the watch and the chain. From a quick, astute start, she almost had me telling her my life story."

In that instance the appearance and demeanour of her subject gave significant clues. But in radio interviews she couldn't see her subjects. This was a hideous challenge. My mother once refused to interview a woman in the *As It Happens* studio until the woman took off her dark sunglasses. By concealing her eyes she was intentionally depriving the interviewer of an important source of information. Since most of *As It Happens'* interviews were conducted on the telephone, it was as if everyone was wearing dark sunglasses. There are some advantages to this. You can take notes, you need not feign rapt attention, you are emboldened to ask harder questions. ("What chances an interviewer can take when he's hundreds, maybe thousands of miles away!" my mother once wrote.) But you must also determine a subject's mood, personality, vulnerabilities from the voice alone. This was among my mother's greatest skills.

"I find myself almost physically in love with everyone on the phone," she wrote. "I have often felt that radio is the most democratic medium, because you can't tell if someone's short, fat, or ugly. Every day I madly leap across this chasm where the person being interviewed doesn't know you and you don't know them. You realize then how beautiful so many voices are."

As It Happens was about everything and anything. A typical show was composed of about one-third Canadian stories, one-third international, and one-third goofy. As versatile as she was, it was the goofy stories she loved best: the man who ate live crabs, for example. For this interview, she had the brilliant notion of, in effect, interviewing the crab first. The creature was allowed to crawl and thump all over the microphone, giving listeners an acute sense of its vitality; then her guest was invited to crunch its squirming head off.

No national leader fascinated her more than the strongman who wanted to catapult himself across a river with the help of twenty dwarfs; or the 370-pound spaghetti champion who escaped from his fat farm to maintain his title; or the world's tallest girl (seven feet, five inches); or the grower of a giant cabbage. And, it would seem, her taste reflected that of her listeners. "I'm never told our coverage of Lebanon was super," she wrote. "It's always, 'Hey, that King Kong guy crying in the phone booth in Chicago — what an item!'"

The show was more than a showcase for lunatics however. In its heyday, *As It Happens* broke many important stories.

"There was a time when *As It Happens* was on the front page of the *Globe* every week," says Max Allen (perhaps exaggerating slightly). "One example is an item we did about lead poisoning in Toronto. While we were broadcasting it, lawyers walked into the studio with a court injunction setting out which things we couldn't broadcast. So Starowicz did a brilliant thing, which was to read the injunction on the air, which just got us into endless trouble. It was front page news for weeks."

My mother belonged to that journalistic school which believes objectivity is possible. She was dedicated to the idea of fairness. "In five years of almost nightly interviews about murder and mayhem in the Middle East, I've tried to be calm, flat, and cool in asking questions about the day's events, even though often I'm in pain and in passionate disagreement with the person on the other end. No matter how many letters go to the president of the CBC suggesting that I'm a Zionist agent with 'ingenious techniques' and an 'insatiable appetite for propaganda'; no matter how much my phone rings at home because some irate Jewish listener wants to ask me, 'What kind of Jew are you to be sympathetic to the Arabs?', I've got a very clear conscience about my 'even-handedness' on this most difficult of political dilemmas."

She would boast that she had "no respect whatsoever for authority." Prime ministers and popes "are just the same quivering pieces of flesh we all are," she frequently observed.

"I would like to think that most of the interviews I do are conducted in an atmosphere of cordiality and even warmth. But every once in a while something in the voice — something in the sound of an answer — gets to me. The adrenalin surges, and before I realize it I'm going for broke: what makes him think he can get that one by me?"

Much stamina was required to do *As It Happens*. Max Allen, one of four producers who was there when my mother was hired, outlasted forty-three others. As he explains, "Today, a story meeting at *Sunday Morning* can last three hours. Our story meetings were ten minutes long. These weren't story meetings so much as emergency councils. All the producers knew what the show had to sound like, and that we had to have ninety minutes of it. We didn't spend a lot of time discussing it."

"It got very competitive between the two shows," Peter Gzowski remembers. "We were both too much over our heads at the beginning to compete. Starowicz is a very smart general — he encouraged that kind of competition. It became like the *Tely* and the *Star* had been — it was wonderful for both of us. It was probably the friendliest of competitions but we really were at each other. We tried to steal phone numbers and we would do stories just so that they wouldn't. We all kind of liked each other, so it wasn't, 'those bastards at *As It Happens*', but Mark, every time they made a headline he'd pin it up on the wall. Both programs had a wonderful sense of unit — esprit de program."

"Esprit de program," as Gzowski puts it, is an immeasurable yet essential element of a good show. Twenty years later, at CBC TV's ill-fated *Prime Time News*, there was an unmistakable air of depression and alienation. At *As It Happens* there was electricity in the air, almost a giddiness.

Although much of the show was pre-taped, producers had short deadlines — often unreasonably short — to get the pieces edited for the air. Their edited pieces would often be finished only moments before they ran. Between 5:30 and 7:00 p.m. the stairway of the radio building became a very dangerous place. Story producers hurtled from the editing rooms on the second floor, to studio F on the first. It must have annoyed them to see a child in the way as they frantically rushed past. In my eyes, they exuded purpose and heroism.

(All of this action is lost at *As It Happens* today. In the new CBC headquarters, producers no longer run an obstacle course to get to the studio, which is located adjacent to their offices.)

Veterans of the show speak nostalgically about it, and nothing moves them more than memories of the camaraderie. Max Allen recalls: "We had an institution called 'The Good Mornings'. You would arrive at your desk and someone would have left a clipping attached to the words, 'Good Morning'. Starowicz was real interested in bus plunge stories. You know: 'Bus plunge kills 53 in India'; 'Bus plunge kills 10 in Mexico'. Somebody else was really into missing digits — people having their fingers and toes cut off. Barbara went through a hippo stage, so she got clippings on that. Sometimes these were put on the air. That kind of humour was an important part of the program."

As much as she hated interviewing celebrities, my mother herself became one, perhaps thanks to one interview more than any other: a March 1979 encounter with Harold Ballard, owner of the Toronto Maple Leafs.

"Women belong horizontal on their backs and should only be allowed to stand up once in a while," Ballard bellowed to my mother after she made a sarcastic remark about the poor performance of the Leafs that year. Then he hung up on her. His outrageous remarks made my mother a feminist heroine because she maintained her humour throughout the exchange. She read a letter to Ballard on the air the next day, forgiving him, since he was already "suffering enough" as the owner of the Leafs. Anyway, she added, she knew she was his favourite "BROADcaster". A few months later when she won the 1979 ACTRA award for best radio interviewer, she held up her statuette to the crowd and said: "Thank you, Harold."

The image thus bolstered was tarnished — quite unfairly — by what we can only call "the curtsy affair". In 1982, the summer after my mother's first season on *The Journal,* she was asked to cover a royal tour with Lloyd Robertson, then still with the CBC. *The Globe and Mail* reported that my mother, upon meeting the Queen, refused to curtsy to her.

McKenzie Porter fumed in the *Toronto Sun,* "Women who refuse to curtsy to the Queen as Barbara Frum refused last week, insult not solely her Majesty but you and me and all our neighbours. Such churlishness usually characterizes the uneducated woman, the woman who confuses the person and the office of the sovereign."

The *Times-Colonist* in Victoria, B.C. editorialized: "It is strange that such an intelligent person cannot distinguish between being civil and servile."

A letter to the editor in the *Toronto Star* suggested that my mother be guillotined. A letter to *The Journal* written by a dental surgeon suggested with slightly more restraint that she be fired: "For heaven's sake, kick that hatchet-faced nincompoop off *The Journal.* She is not a true Canadian — and she is not a lady. Refused to curtsy to the Queen. She is nauseating."

This was how my mother explained the whole situation in an interview she later gave me for my book, *The Newsmakers:*

At the start of every Royal Tour there is a reception that is put on by the Palace where the Queen shakes the hand of every journalist who is accredited to cover the tour. It seemed to me a rather obvious gesture: trying to get good coverage and good spirit about the tour — give them a free glass of wine and let them meet the Queen.

It's very patronizing the way they do it. You are held in an enormous holding room until she and Prince Philip are in place. You are told what to wear: gloves. You are told to not touch her. Or put out your hand. It's her gesture to make.

Allan Fotheringham and Elizabeth Gray were heckling me as we were all practising our curtsies. Fotheringham was teasing me because he knew what an obstreperous type I was and he was quizzing me as to what I was going to do. And I said within the hearing of [*Globe and Mail* reporter] Nora McCabe — 'I don't curtsy to anyone' (which is basically my philosophy of life). She put it in the paper. And she got me into a lot of trouble.

In the end I'm sure I did something funny with my foot although I wouldn't call it a curtsy. I was perfectly respectful however. I just didn't like to be told how to behave to another mortal. I have respect for the Queen but to me, as one woman to another, it didn't make any sense at all.

Still, my mother acquired a reputation as an anti-monarchist, and on that 1982 tour, when she was sitting in a press box at a stadium in Calgary, an especially devoted royal subject clawed his way across ceiling-mounted banners and bunting to reach my mother and beg her: "Please, Barbara, don't say anything nasty about the Queen!"

The truth was that of all the people in the universe she dreamed of interviewing, the Queen topped the list.

It tickled my mother to discover that one of her favourite performers, singer k.d. lang, held similar fantasies. My mother told me,

"I'm crazy about k.d. lang . . . so when I interviewed her for *The Journal* and she said she wanted to sing a duet with the Queen, I really laughed. I thought: here we are, two small-town Canadian girls with the same old aspiration. I want to sing with the Queen too. I imagine a lot of hard-working women empathize with the Queen."

Seldom has any news show become as entirely identified with its anchor as *As It Happens* did. How identified? A formal apology in March 1977, from Trina McQueen, the executive producer of the *National News* to Bob Campbell, then producer of *As It Happens*, says it best:

> You called me yesterday to complain that *As It Happens* hadn't been given proper credit on *The National* for the interviews with the gunman and the hostage. I agree with you that we should have mentioned the program name rather than the host. There was no technical reason for this. . . . It was simply this: the editors involved honestly felt that mentioning Barbara Frum's name was a proper credit. Her name, as you know, has become almost interchangeable with the show, as in "I heard it on Barbara Frum last night."

At the beginning of the struggle

Chapter 8

The Dread Word

BARBARA FRUM:

If this was the age of duels, you'd be dead ten times
by now.

NORMAN MAILER:

Well, there are worse things than being dead, you know.

BARBARA FRUM:

Like what?

NORMAN MAILER:

Dying slowly. Shamelessly, shamefully, and without honour.
Or of an awful disease.

BARBARA FRUM:

I'm glad you added that.

THE JOURNAL, *April 1983*

FOR THE FIFTEEN YEARS that I knew about my mother's
leukemia, I honoured her request not to talk about it. She couldn't
bear the thought of a public reputation as "that sick woman who
does television." And she feared that if news of her ill-health were
leaked, it would be detrimental to the career that she believed
helped to keep her alive.

But now that her battle is over, I am releasing myself from my agreement with her. I want to share the truth of how brave she remained despite her fears, how dignified despite her anxieties. When my mother died, my father said that the word that best described her was "noble". Never was she more noble than in her long struggle with death.

I understand, and she especially understood, that thousands of people travel this same route every day, honourably fulfilling their duties despite tremendous physical and emotional burdens. On her optimistic days, my mother would cheer herself, and others suffering from disease who sought her comfort, with the thought: "We're just the same as everyone else — the only difference is that we know what is going to kill us." But more truthfully, my mother's illness did set her apart. It made her wiser, deeper, more open to love and to living. It brought terrible darkness to her life, but by making those who loved her so acutely aware of her delicacy and preciousness, it also touched her life with light.

Along with worry and fear, weekly doctors' appointments and blood tests, came a profound understanding of how frail is a human being. It was that understanding that transformed her from a person of ordinary sympathy to someone of extraordinary compassion. It brought a sharper insight to her work as an interviewer.

My mother told me the story only once of how she found she had leukemia, almost twenty years ago. You only need to hear such a story once. This is how it is stored in my memory:

One late afternoon in the fall of 1974, after a day of recording interviews at *As It Happens*, and just before an evening out with my father, my thirty-six-year-old mother made time for her annual check-up, a routine act in an organized life. She and her gynecologist had a warm rapport, and as she lay down on his examining table, they began to chat. The doctor wearily told her that he had just had one of the worst days of his career: he had diagnosed two of his patients with breast cancer. He was heartbroken. It made him hate his job. He couldn't wait to go home and have a drink.

"How awful it must be for you to have to tell women they have cancer," said my mother in genuine horror. "I just can't imagine . . ."

"All I can say," replied the doctor, "is that thank God I am now examining a healthy young woman like you!"

A few moments later, he found a large lump in my mother's armpit. The diagnosis of leukemia followed almost immediately. My mother's reaction was bitter shock of the sort that could be expected from someone who until then had possessed faith in the ordered justice of the world. "I'm a good person," she reasoned. "I've always taken care of myself. I don't smoke. I'm not a drinker. I lead a healthy life. How could this happen to me?" Fairness, justice, and order were words she would never use the same way again.

My father's memories of that shattering night revolve around one moment. He picked up my mother after her doctor's appointment to take her to a party at a friend's house. She told my father about the doctor's devastating discovery, and soon they found themselves parked in front of the house where the party was being held, the motor running to keep them warm, unable to move, weeping. "We talked about the diagnosis, how her life was at an end, the poor young babies. I fell apart." Through his sobs my father's resolve surfaced. "I told her that none of us knows how long we have on this earth. We couldn't stop our lives and wait for her to die. I told her life's for living, and that's what we're going to do." To prove his point my father insisted that they had to go inside to the party. They had to carry on as normally as possible. He does not pretend that they had a great time. My mother caught sight of her friend, the writer, W. O. Mitchell, and sat with him in a corner, telling her dreadful news. But even on that night, a steely stoicism was forged: there would be no surrender.

It wasn't that simple of course. "There's this rabbinical saying that you don't hurry to relieve a person of their grief," says June Call-wood. "Grief is work and Barbara worked her grief to the bone."

She did so by leaning heavily on June, a famously compassionate woman whose writing on the subjects of illness, death, and mourning, made her the ideal counsel for a "talking cure". June did not volunteer for this role, she was appointed, and, at times, it wore her out.

"She told me about her leukemia the day after her diagnosis, and for about two or three months after that, she called several times a day," June remembers. "I began to fear that she wasn't going to recover emotionally from the shock, let alone physically. The physical diagnosis was bad enough but what she was doing to herself emotionally — the despair. Deep, deep, despair.

"She was very verbal with me, and sometimes, on my end of the telephone, I thought she was not paying a lot of attention to what it was doing to my life taking five telephone calls a day for months. And I was not flagging in my responsibilities, but I'd be busy, and the phone would ring, and I'd say, 'Oh! I hope that isn't Barbara.' And it would be. And it's not that I resented it but there was so much of it. I don't think I'm exaggerating to say it was five times a day. Then, it stopped just like that. All of a sudden she had enough of the grief and she moved on. It didn't fade away, it was just totally over."

In the days after the initial diagnosis, my parents sought out the best medical opinions. The leading expert at Princess Margaret Hospital in Toronto told my mother to get her affairs in order: she wouldn't have more than a year. Unsatisfied with this dismal verdict, she continued to search out doctors until she found one who thought five years was possible. She enlisted his services.

My mother shared the news of her diagnosis with everyone at *As It Happens*, but it was to Mark Starowicz and Margaret Lyons that she expressed her desire to continue in her job. Margaret Lyons recalls asking her if she really thought that's what would be best, and when my mother reaffirmed, Margaret agreed that she should continue, but must apprise them of any serious developments.

David was thirteen, I eleven, and Matthew six at the time of my mother's diagnosis, and our parents decided to keep the news from us until each turned sixteen. They feared the consequences of our knowing we had a weak mother. For their daughter, especially, they wanted the way clear for a classically Freudian early adolescence in which I could reject my mother without hindrance, an unnecessary precaution since I never did rebel.

I also believe that by not telling us, my parents engaged in a subtle act of hope. And indeed, I consider it the great miracle of my life that I did not lose my mother while still a child, as she feared might happen.

In 1976, two summers into her care of her disease, my mother decided to send David and me to National Music Camp in Michigan. At thirteen, I was exactly the same age as she had been when she was shipped off to a depressing summer at the same place. The difference was, that while Florence had organized my mother's departure with military efficiency, David and I had only a few weeks' notice before we were frantically packed off to study drama, dance, and song — for none of which either of us had shown the slightest aptitude. I took at face value the explanation my mother gave me: "It will be good for you to be around all those talented kids," she said, holding no illusions about my artistic gifts. As I understand now, however, our mother was preparing us for the more permanent separation she feared was imminent.

For the first three days at camp, the first serious separation I had ever had from my mother, I cried myself silly in the infirmary. I was paralyzed with fear, and the longing to be with my mother, a foreshadowing of the way I would spend the rest of my adolescence once I learned of my mother's leukemia.

Almost as if according to my mother's plans, my relationship with my brother changed forever that summer. Until then, my brother viewed me as the most unforgivable mistake my parents had ever committed. But when left alone to care for me in my misery, he responded with fraternal tenderness. He checked on me daily, indulging me with inspiring pep talks, buying me heaps of ice cream from the Melody Freeze, and helping me find courage.

My mother was greatly relieved that this macabre "dress rehearsal" came off so well, as she hinted in letters laced with nuances we didn't comprehend:

> Dear David,
>   Linny wrote to say how wonderful you've been to her and we're so pleased and proud to hear that — kind of relieved too — because we know someday you two are going to need each other even more.

To me she wrote:

> For you to experience your own capacities by testing them out in a kind of difficult, sometimes lonely but protected place — well I'm so glad you had that chance now and that we could give you that experience.

In another letter to David:

> I'm writing to you and Linda now just because I'm feeling all sentimental and miss you very much. I know we'll probably see each other before this arrives, but I'm so full of feelings of love and admiration and pride in you I have to spill them somewhere. . . . Murray's been congratulating me all summer for sending you to camp — for realizing this was the moment

for you to have a sharp break in routine, to send you out where you could discover more about yourself and what you are and will be than you ever could have been surrounded by all the normal clutter of the rest of the year. Summer is for breaking out. For trying on things. For even trying on some pain. . . . We sent you [to camp] to give you an experience, a chance to be a little lonely, a little giddy, a little cocky, a little uncertain all at the same time. Someday you'll be completely on your own. Not yet thank God, I'm not ready yet.

To me:

Murray and I were talking about this summer for you and what we hope you'll get out of it. We're hoping that once you see what can be accomplished in an isolated couple of months — 8 weeks, that's all — that you will have a better appreciation of our constant harping about productive time. It's been our experience that the pressure of time makes people more efficient and more appreciative of fleeting moments and opportunities. People with too much time are wasteful, lazy and unproductive. They think they'll always get down to something worthwhile tomorrow. I hope when you see what talented, hard-working people can accomplish that you will dedicate yourself to developing your own gifts.

Her letters were full of emotion: deep sadness and maternal love. We didn't know that they were also tinged with dread of death. To David:

You have to find your own way to feeling that your life means something. You also have to find your own way of living with the ultimate pain that no individual's life really means anything in the end. That's where humour comes in . . . to laugh at your fate even while you're doing it. To marvel at the complexities. And the absurdity of certainty. And yet to believe in order.

To me:

> When you're away, the heart of the house is gone somehow. You probably are so busy living inside Linda Frum, you don't even know how important your life is to other people.

To shield our innocence from the dark cloud, our parents were vigilant in keeping any word of my mother's sickness out of the press. Within a couple of weeks of her original diagnosis, Blaik Kirby, the *Globe and Mail*'s television critic, called my father at his office to say that he had heard of my mother's fatal illness and wanted the story confirmed for his column.

"I told him that I wouldn't confirm or deny the story," my father remembers. "But I wanted to examine with him why he was doing this. What possible benefits could be obtained by it?"

My father laid on the pressure. "I asked him, 'How many inches will this take in your column Mr. Kirby? Will it take a half an inch? An inch? And with that amount of space you're going to destroy the lives of my children, you are going to interfere with Barbara's ability to work.' And then I asked him, 'Who knows how long anybody lives? Nobody really knows the span of life we have. That's what keeps us going. If you knew the day, you would just curl up and wait for it. Is she going to die? Yes. But we're all going to die. You have no story there.'"

Either my father was especially persuasive that day, or Blaik Kirby was an unusually sensitive newspaper man, or both. Kirby agreed not to run the story. The poor man died himself suddenly, only one year later, of a heart attack.

If at first my parents wanted to keep the truth about my mother's illness out of the press for our sake, later my mother developed a superstitious obsession with preserving secrecy. Perhaps secrecy is not the word: in the aftermath of her diagnosis, my mother told her friends about it and word spread rapidly. Many Canadians knew she was ill. But she had a horror of seeing the truth in type.

Before her 1974 interview with Heather Robertson for the book, *Her Own Woman,* my mother made Robertson promise to omit any mention of her leukemia. "It was like witchcraft for her," remembers Robertson. "She thought that if it got out, it would come true. It was a spiritual thing. If it was kept secret, she would be okay."

Fortunately, Robertson had no interest in disclosing the information, not only because she respected my mother's privacy, but because such a disclosure was out of harmony with the thesis of her essay, which was the emergence of female power in society. "We were all very aware of how vulnerable women were to attack," recalls Robertson. "She was vulnerable enough. She didn't want to make herself more vulnerable. This would feed into her image as a weaker vessel."

Not all reporters were as sympathetic. Charlotte Gray asked to have her name removed from a *Chatelaine* "Woman of the Year" profile she wrote about my mother in 1983 after the magazine's editor, Mildred Istona, complied with my mother's request to pull the paragraphs Gray had written divulging the truth about my mother's leukemia. I'm told that Istona still agonizes about whether she did the right thing. Charlotte Gray remembers that when she did a second *Chatelaine* article on my mother in 1985, in which references to leukemia were again omitted, she felt angry and compromised.

"Barbara discussed her leukemia with me, answered all my questions about it but told me she would be very unhappy if I wrote about it," Gray remembers. "She never told me I couldn't write it. She said she would leave it to my judgment, and appealed to my sense of honour. She was a very smart lady. She understood my psychology and knew that if she put it to me that way, I wouldn't do it. But nonetheless I felt very manipulated. As a journalist, my sense of professionalism was compromised. My colleagues, who knew about her leukemia were very hard on me when the piece came out, like the editor from *Toronto Life* who said, 'I see you missed the story on Barbara Frum.'"

Heather Robertson understood and respected my mother's motivation. "She may not have had the *Journal* job if the public knew she had leukemia. She was very astute about controlling her image. She did not want people to know that she was sick, nor that she was rich."

"Did anyone ever break the story?" Gray asked me from her temporary home in Boston, where she was living around the time of my mother's death.

"Yes," I told her, "Stephen Godfrey, in the *Globe and Mail,* two months before she died."

"There you go," said Gray, as aware of my mother's superstitious fears as Heather Robertson had been. "That's just how she imagined it would be."

The onset of my mother's disease coincided with the rise of my father's fortunes in the real estate business. By 1972, he had completely given up his dental practice and had built his first shopping centre, in Hamilton, Ontario. By 1974 he was building three new shopping centres a year.

But my mother did not allow either of these drastic developments to alter their lives. She avoided fad remedies. She drank as much coffee and ate as much red meat as she wished, and since she hadn't exercised before, she didn't start then. Nor did she try to live it up.

However, trips to Europe did become more frequent (as many as three a year), and she did have a weakness for impulse buying (which she made up for by being frugal and sensible most of the time).

On a 1974 trip to Paris, my newly successful father encouraged my mother to browse inside the House of Christian Dior. It was summer and they had a sale on fur coats. The first one she saw was made of monkey fur. It was unlike anything she had ever seen before. It looked like bursts of black flowers. "She tried it on," my father recalls, "and she looked smashing in it. It was so wonderful, I bought it on the spot."

Most of the time she feared her wealth might alienate her from the people she most wanted to spend time with. She was delighted when anyone writing a profile mentioned that she was "married to a dentist."

In a 1976 letter from the French Riviera town, Beaulieu-Sur-Mer, she told me:

> We've had a couple of good days here. It's very pretty. The pool is huge and excellent. The rooms are very nice. But for some reason I feel like I'm play acting. Do you know the feeling? You're going through motions that look good on the outside but eventually the phoniness of 'dressing for dinner' and being waited on hand and foot by attentive waiters gets to you.
>
> I'm obviously meant to be a working person in this world, not a fancy grande dame who swoons on luxury.

Her disease took away my mother's easy mirth and optimism, but gave her back the wisdom and gentleness that were part of her appeal. "There are only so many raspberry seasons in a life," she would say in what became a guiding principle. She could see through the shallow trappings of success, and by doing so became more sensitive, modest, and approachable. "Heaven gives its favourites early death," wrote Lord Byron.

In the immediate hours after my mother died, I had no idea what to do with myself. As many times as I had lived the moment of her death in my mind, I had never imagined the sixty minutes after. What do you *do* with yourself?

Eventually, desperately, I reached for a book I hadn't looked at in fifteen years. It was my mother's 1976 book, *As It Happened*, the only one she ever wrote despite almost annual offers from publishers.

At the time, I had strongly resented the book's demanding presence in my mother's life. It was supposed to be a straight-forward project, a simple collection of her best interviews. But, as was her way, my mother poured herself into it, attempting to infuse the book with as much personality, humour and insight as possible. "I don't think I could take doing a book; working towards a climax of judgment would absolutely kill me," she had told Heather Robertson the year before.

But she did take on a book. Although the judgments didn't kill her — on the whole they were favourable — the writing of it did take much of her psychic energy. As she exclaimed to David in a letter she wrote the summer before it was published: "That damn book just wasn't worth what it did to me."

She was operating under a "Jack McClelland deadline", which, as Robert Fulford defined it, meant that "Jack commissioned the book on Thursday and wanted it by Saturday." Every spare moment of her evenings and weekends were dedicated to it.

For all the pain that book caused me in that lonely year, it seemed worthwhile on the night of her death. Her written journalism was produced in an era before it was acceptable for journalists to inject themselves into their stories. She gave away little of herself there. But in the book, she is present on every page.

These are some of the words that comforted me in the long hours after. They are from a chapter of the book entitled, "Surviving":

In October 1972, a party of young Uruguayan rugby players crashed in the frozen peaks of the Andes while flying to a match in Chile. They were lost for seventy days, until two of the hardiest and bravest managed to climb out of those desolate mountains and lead rescuers to their helpless comrades. A year later the two young heroes were in North America to publicize the book Alive, which told their story. The book was a best-seller, not just because it described an extraordinary adventure, but because it vividly spelled out how the boys had refused to die of starvation and survived by eating the flesh of those who had been killed on impact. There were many people at the time who condemned the survivors, suggesting that cannibalism was too terrible an act to be condoned — which struck me as pretty pious. It was like saying that the boys should have died there, so that we could have praised them for their nobility. For me, the fact of cannibalism was only a distracting — although admittedly bizarre — detail, really only a symbol of what human beings are prepared to do to live.

When Nando Parrado and Roberto Canessa became available for interview, I decided to down-play the obvious and ghoulish aspects. Instead, I thought I'd concentrate on the psychological choices of staying alive, and on what they'd learned on that mountain about themselves and others. All had not been generosity and self-sacrifice among the Andes survivors. In fact, their survival had involved some pretty selfish and unheroic things. I wanted to hear about those aspects and about the kind of character it takes to keep on going in a seemingly hopeless situation.

Unfortunately, I got to talk to Parrado and Canessa only after they had become veterans of the talk-show circuit and had learned how to handle interviewers. As they came bustling into our New York studio, I could overhear them on the line — friendly, vital, easy-going young men, clearly enjoying the attention they were getting. About fifteen minutes into the interview, after it became obvious that the boys had turned the drama of their suffering into a pat performance, I hesitantly asked, "Would you be offended if I wondered if finally a human being doesn't have to be a bit of a bastard to survive a terrible event — if maybe saints don't make it?" Before I could establish whether they had understood what I was getting at, Canessa responded in the same humble, earnest manner he'd used in answering all my other questions.

"No. I think you must be a warm man to survive, because although I was suffering, if I'd died there, I would have felt that I'd tried my best for everybody."

It was a sweet answer but it didn't explain how people survive any better than had the rest of our conversation; although it struck me as interesting that it was Canessa, the domineering and difficult one on the mountain, who had answered, rather than Parrado, who was described as spoiled and thoughtless before the tragedy, but in crisis came as close as a human being can to selflessness.

Anyway, I let the subject drop and, after a few more exchanges, I said, 'I wish you both good luck,' to signal that I was about to sign off the line. Canessa, however, wasn't finished with me. The moment he thought we were off the air he jumped in hard.

"Do you still think we are bastards?" he demanded.

"I am sorry, Mr. Canessa," I answered uneasily. "You see, that's the trouble. What right have I got to stand in judgment of you? It's just that we all identify so much with you and what you've suffered. And we feel tormented because we fear that we would be no good at all."

"You feel that way?" he repeated, unsatisfied. And again I tried to explain what I had meant.

"You see, we're struggling to understand how a human being could have the strength to put up with what you did. Do you see?"

"But I think if we were just animals there," he answered quietly, "if we just think of ourselves, we would have killed each other in a fight, or each one go his own way. But we are human beings. I think that's the reason why it worked."

And then he really let me have it.

"But I appreciate very much that you are sincere and you told me your feeling. I always fight for people to say what they feel. Not only nice things." And, with that, he stood up and walked out of the studio, but not before all that pique and pain and hostility had gone out over the air. To this moment I still feel some guilt for demanding introspection. Parrado and Canessa didn't owe me — or anybody — an accounting of their thoughts or motives. Of course, I remain fascinated by who survives and how they do so, and I always have been..."

It is written in the Psalms: "Teach us to number our days that we may apply our hearts with wisdom." My mother understood; and it is what she taught us.

Barbara with Matthew in the backyard

Chapter 9

At Home With Barbara

BARBARA FRUM:

I think I like you, Miss Vanek

JOANN VANEK:

No kidding, Why?

BARBARA FRUM:

Because I haven't noticed the workload going down, either.

JOANN VANEK:

Are you married, Barbara?

BARBARA FRUM:

Am I ever.

JOANN VANEK:

How many kids?

BARBARA FRUM:

Three. And two dogs.

JOANN VANEK:

And a full-time job and a full house, not an apartment?

BARBARA FRUM:

Correct.

JOANN VANEK:

That's a lot of work.

BARBARA FRUM:

And a nervous breakdown. That takes a day a week.

AS IT HAPPENS, *November 1974*
Interview with Joann Vanek, American researcher
on the subject of Superwomen

To ENTER the vibrant work force — and pay housekeepers to look after the children — this was pure progress to many of my mother's contemporaries. "We were not working because we had to, we were working because we wanted to," Geraldine Sherman remembers. "There was a lot of discussion about what to do after you had a baby."

My generation has come to feel a sense of dissatisfaction as powerful as anything recorded by Betty Friedan as we worry whether our work short-changes our children. But, for my mother's peers, work was liberation. They could think of no reason to view it as anything else. The educated and civilized women who had preceded them — women like my grandmother Florence although, oddly enough, not Florence herself — were frustrated by exclusion from the "real" world. My mother's generation was determined not to repeat the mistakes of their mothers. As my mother later joked, they wanted to make new mistakes of their own.

In the late sixties and early seventies, however, joking was not allowed. My mother and her friends showed a limitless optimism that women could work full-time, raise happy children, and maintain fulfilling sexual and romantic relationships. In an article for *Maclean's* in 1968, my mother described her idea of the new woman. She was writing about Ph.D. candidates with young children in tow.

There's a new kind of academic woman on campuses and she's young, chic, and decorative. She wears short skirts and patterned stockings and she's handy with an eyebrow pencil. She diapers her babies, makes a creditable Boeuf Bourguignon, wears a hostess skirt when she entertains and, when she bares her mind in public, men pay attention.

Three years after that *Maclean's* article, my mother insisted even more stubbornly that women owed their first loyalty to themselves. When Margaret Sinclair married Prime Minister Trudeau in 1971, my mother was scathing. She told a reporter, "She's imprisoned with three choices: Skiing, Skating, or Bicycling. But she has chosen that way of life. Her personal happiness does not depend on my approval, but for any young girl to give up her independence to that extent, it's an insult."

Everything in women's lives needed to be challenged. It was part of my mother's genius to reflect the passions and convictions of her times — often more knowledgeably and intelligently than they deserved. Although she would later deride her feminist phase as "those six months in 1969 when we were mad at everybody," for many years she championed the women's movement.

At a 1971 speaking engagement, she suggested that communal soup kitchens might be an attractive time-saving device for the working mother. "It's just as easy to feed twenty kids as it is to feed four. And I'd just as soon have a dozen children in my basement for one Sunday afternoon, then have three Sundays free, as have three children there every week."

I am confident that ten minutes after this suggestion came out of her mouth, its ridiculousness began to strike her. Replying to the question, "Are you a feminist?" put to her by a student journalist for a University of Toronto publication in 1981, she said,

> *The Feminine Mystique* brought [the feminist movement] to everyone's attention. . . . We all got angry and then we all

calmed down. Like every pendulum it went too far, and then it started to swing back. It seems to me that we all woke up and we realized it was a middle-class movement for middle-class women who could have housekeepers and glamorous jobs . . . jobs for self-fulfillment. We suddenly realized then that we had been very self-centred. And where women were exploited, was in so many other places . . . We were wallowing in self-pity.

There are still traces of this self-pity in a letter to David in 1976, when he was sixteen:

I remember watching my [own] mother get us off to camp each summer, working till three or four in the morning behind a mound of clothes on the dining-room table and actually think-ing — "Well, what else are mothers for? I didn't ask to be born. She had me, now it's her job to look after me." Well, parents are forlorn, frightened, pleasure-seeking animals too. They've unwittingly surrendered enormous freedom at the moment of maybe their finest glory — when that first child was born. And each addition is a glorious but heavy responsibility.

My mother was trying to lighten responsibilities to her chil-dren so that she might play a role as the equal of my father. She assumed — sometimes too easily — that so long as her children were loved, and their material needs met, their vagrant whims could be ignored. But by the time she got to *The Journal,* she had begun to understand that this denial of the demands of motherhood served women ill. As she told Susan Crean in 1985:

At *The Journal,* the women work extraordinarily hard at prov-ing they are not distracted [by children, family, husbands] and I don't notice the men have that problem. It's the men who talk about their babies and are always saying they have to go home to tend to a sick child. It's unbelievably funny. I rarely make quips like this, but one holiday Monday recently I came in the office and exclaimed, "How come it's women's night on *The Journal*?" All the men had disappeared for the long weekend and the women were putting out the program. Even Starowicz had checked himself off because he had to do the gardening and look after his family. I think women are penalized by that and still feel constrained. Men are not ashamed to say they have a sick child or have to go home because their wives will be angry if they are late another night. It has almost become chic for men to use their children as an excuse to get out of here.

But in the seventies my mother threw herself as wholeheartedly into her work as the toughest of those *Journal* producers of the eighties. She had to prove that she could subordinate her parental instincts as uncompromisingly as any man. And perhaps she genuinely did have to prove it — not merely to the satisfaction of the era's remaining male chauvinists, but to far more ruthless judges — her feminist colleagues, who looked to my mother to set a standard.

Margaret Lyons, her boss at CBC Radio and a mother herself, approved of this approach. "My view in those days was that women had to make a choice whether to stay home and look after their families, or if they wanted to work, get themselves a professional, live-in nanny," she said. "A lot of women were very sloppy about it. They fussed about whether their teenage babysitter was going to show up or not. And I would say, 'you are earning good money; you should stop worrying about it and get a really good professional nanny, and while you're here think about work and stop phoning home every few minutes, because if that's how you feel, you should be at home.' One of the things I admired about Barbara was that she could sort things out that way. She worried about important things, but not whether or not [her children] were being fed properly."

I don't think my mother ever did sacrifice her children to the feminist revolution. She had a secret insurance policy: as a woman of the fifties, she had married and given birth rather early. When she accepted the job as host of *As It Happens* at age thirty-four, David was already eleven, and I was almost nine. We never saw the inside of a day-care centre, an institution that horrified my mother. There was enough money to pay for full-time, live-in help. More importantly, my father supported her ambitions and willingly became a pioneering modern dad.

When we had trouble at school, or any need at all, it was agreed family policy that we call our father. Our mother also had a "put my children through no matter what" telephone policy, but our reason for calling had better be *really important*. Our father we could bug for any old thing. "Murr, my period hurts so much I think I'm going to faint! Can you please tell the nurse it's okay for me to go home?" Since these calls didn't ruffle my father, I learned not to let them ruffle me.

Music recitals, school plays, parent-teacher nights, were my father's domain. Not that he was hanging around in slippers and a shaggy sweater all day: we understood that with construction sites to visit and interest rates on the brain, he was a busy man. When he came to school, he came looking every bit the dynamic executive, outfitted in the ultra-sharp, wide-lapelled suits of the period. There was a limit to his New-Age inclinations.

Most of the time, though, we were in the care of a series of live-in housekeepers. If one of these women stayed with us for more than two years, my parents considered it a miracle. My mother was a good employer, paying better than average wages and taking a personal interest in our housekeepers' lives. But, as she would cry after each of them left, it didn't pay.

In a letter I received one summer, my mother reported hopefully on her latest employee:

Hopi is working out well, quite tidy, but best news — she's
a very good cook! A different recipe from our books every
night. But modest quantities so you won't get fat. I'm sure
you'll like this one. A great relief for us all.

All I can say is that this letter was written when I was sixteen,
and when I re-read it, I didn't even recall a housekeeper named
Hopi. She musn't have lasted the summer. Few of the housekeepers
bonded with our family. And although some were warm and loving, others were surly and indifferent.

One vivid memory David and I share: As young school children we were on strict orders from our mother not to cross the
major intersection that separated our grade school from our home
until the housekeeper-of-the-moment came to guide us. Twice a
day, at lunch and after school, we would walk to this point and
stand shoulder to shoulder, silently staring at our warm house, so
tantalizingly close. We'd wait and wait, pull our hands into our
snowsuits and curl our toes inside our boots. Often the street would
be barren of traffic and yet, obediently, we would stand, pathetically
following mother's orders. It was not unusual for the housekeeper
to become so engrossed in her soap opera that she would forget us
altogether. As our noses and toes froze we could not help grum-
bling: "Why does Mummy have to work?"

But, as my mother would surely point out, we became independent children. We cooked our own breakfasts, catering to our
own palates. David enjoyed a daily plate of extra-crispy fried bacon
even though, being eight years old, he almost incinerated himself
each morning. We devised our own homework timetables (or not),
violated our parent's TV regulations with impunity (at least I did;

David was off somewhere memorizing *The History of Civilization*). When boredom overtook us, we tore each other to pieces. Even this last activity would arouse our housekeeper's interest only if our wrestling bodies obstructed her view of the box.

Once we became adolescents, our independence paid more attractive dividends. We were responsible for monitoring our own alcohol intake and were welcome to serve ourselves from the family liquor cabinet (a master stroke of reverse psychology). We set our own curfews, and were encouraged to have friends over for parties — but *only* when our parents were away for the weekend. We never received an allowance: our parents' strange economic policy was to invite us to help ourselves to the contents of our father's wallet whenever we asked. As my mother said of so many of her experiences, including her early marriage: the result should have been catastrophic. Instead, the dangerous liberties we were granted somehow obviated thoughts of teenage rebellion, perhaps because our parents' very elusiveness made us crave their good opinion more than ever. And there was never any doubt of how to win that — or lose it.

"Yes, but..." I can hear the voice of *Codco's* Greg Malone satirically impersonating Barbara Frum. "Are you bitter?"

The answer is absolutely not. My mother made many mistakes — mistakes my brother and I are determined not to repeat. We know that children miss absent parents as much as they say they do. But somehow, even as children, we understood. We knew that she needed her work as desperately as we needed her; we knew that her work was extraordinary, that it mattered to thousands of people. We always admired her and, I think, we always knew how much she loved us.

In 1981, when I was seventeen years old, my mother told *Chatelaine* magazine: "The nurturing process of being a parent to grown children is in some ways more difficult than the earlier stages."

I doubt if that is universally true. I think that in my mother's case, she emerged from a haze of sometimes misguided feminism to gain a more realistic sense of how much time she needed to spend with us. When wishful thinking gave way to this knowledge, she gave herself unstintingly.

My mother and I confronted each other in one especially unpleasant incident when I was fourteen. I had yet to find out how much living my mother was trying to cram into what she knew would be a truncated life. My parents were away in Belgium on one of their frequent trips. I was bored and restless, and generally resentful of my mother's absence. To amuse myself, I scanned my parents' shelves and found a book entitled, *Her Own Woman: Profiles of Ten Canadian Women*. It was written in 1975, the heyday of feminist literature, and, unbeknownst to me, my mother was one of the women profiled. She had not shown this book to me herself. I opened it and read eagerly.

Then I came across this passage:

> I don't quite feel like their mother. I feel like some person living with them. We've never lived for the sake of our kids, we've always lived our own life. We've both got a real sense of the shortness of life. That's one thing Murray learned from me. Do it now. Indulge your feelings now. Eat that meal now. Don't save, don't wait, don't bank on tomorrow. So we live our lives completely according to the moment. I'm beginning to fear for my children that we haven't built enough structure into their lives. I sense maybe there's a craving for ritual we haven't provided. Our kids can't remember when we've always done something. I think maybe we've let them down. The truth is that we've never been willing to sacrifice our lives for them. I don't

know if that's good or bad. We've each harnessed our
lives to such an extent that to harness what little time
we can have together in the service of our children
never made much sense either. But I consider that
selfish of me. So I feel I'll get docked by God for that,
but I'm not willing to stop. I don't defer for the future
what I can have today, and I'm taking pot luck
about tomorrow.

I absolutely hated my mother when I read that. Not willing to
sacrifice her life for me? How dare she! And to advertise it too! I had
no idea, as I fumed and seethed, that the interview in which she
said these things had taken place just after she learned of her leukemia, when she believed she had only months to live.

A week later my parents returned. My brothers ran to the drive-
way to greet their taxi. Not I. I remained belligerently in my room.

When my mother came through the front door I could hear
her say, "Where's Linny? Where's Linny?"

My retribution was coming. I knew it would be only seconds
before I would hear her heels clicking along the ceramic tile towards
me, that she would open my door and say with sweet enthusiasm,
"Linny! Why didn't you come say hello?"

I said "hello" faintly, and returned to the magazine I was flip-
ping through with affected nonchalance.

That would crush her.

After ignoring her for several hours, I decided it was time to
let her know about what I had read. She was not, I was shocked to
discover, apologetic.

The fight that followed was the worst we ever had and we
debated its themes for years afterwards. The bitterness and anger
lingered for months. The ultimate resolution did not come until I
received this letter from her three years later, in August of 1979:

Dear Linny,

This is a letter of apology and a new resolution . . . I
re-read, for the first time, the interview I gave Heather
Robertson for the book *Her Own Woman* — the interview
you took exception to for its references to you.

Of course you were right — you were just focusing
too narrowly on the foolish things I had to say about child-
rearing . . . I'm not now disavowing all my statements. I'm only
conceding to you that written down, the views are too blunt,
too one-dimensional. It's not that I was misquoted, but that I
obviously didn't and wouldn't and couldn't say everything I feel
— about kids, or having you, or working, or journalism, or
being a Jew — and that by saying a few things and omitting
most, I sound like a fool.

In apologizing for doing the interview I must explain and
qualify — for there is one aspect that I am grateful for.

The interview is like a sharp snapshot of me at a very critical moment in my life. Perhaps you see my life as a single
stream, fairly steady, fairly even; perhaps no child can see her
parent's changes, the way she becomes something new (and not
necessarily better I must add), the way we can lose connection
even with the way we were as recently as five years ago . . .

The interview was given by chance and under a great
deal of prodding. If the first person Heather had used had
worked out, she would never have even approached me. But
that explains only the event, and doesn't explain why she got
so much confession out of me, for believe it or not, I really
am more circumspect. But by luck for her, the interview was
done at a moment of intense change for me. It was a period
of almost frantic activity; of intense effort to pack more life
into the time I had; of great psychological effort to subdue
panic about my health and my future; to make a mark; fight

every battle while I could; extract every drop of sweetness that I could.

Reading my statements makes me realize just how much I've changed. I'm not less selfish, just quieter. I'm not less silly, just smarter about keeping my mouth shut.

So that's the part I'm grateful for — the record, however embarrassing. And though it doesn't get at 10% of what I feel about any of the issues raised, it does give off the psychological style and temperature of me at a particular moment in my life...

And so I repeat the apology, and share with you this resolution. No more interviews... There's nothing like seeing your faults cast in cold type to shake you up enough to change.

Love, Mum

As a working mother myself now, I feel more sympathy for the choices my mother made. My father says, "Let's face it, if she was with you as much as you wanted, she would never have been allowed to leave the room." And he's right. I'm sure my mother felt her job was good for us; particularly for me. Her example, she believed, would teach me to appreciate my own potential.

From the youngest age she encouraged me to think freely and broadly about what I wanted to do with my life. Once, around age twelve, I made the monumental mistake of suggesting idly, "it must be fun being a diplomat's wife, going to parties all the time. ..."

Before I could finish speaking the thought, the weight of a thousand bricks crashed down on my head, as my parents said almost in unison: "You'll either be a diplomat *yourself* or nothing at all! Being somebody's wife is not an adequate career goal. Who raised you? What are we teaching you here?" I should stress that my father was even angrier than my mother. "I hate the idea that my little girl might in some way be limited because she's a woman," my father once told a reporter for an article on husbands of career women. "It just doesn't have to be that way and Barbara is living proof of that."

My mother was among the very few who actually discouraged their daughters from acquiring housekeeping skills. On weekends, when the housekeeper of the moment was away, our house would subside into squalor. As I scan memory and imagination, an image of my mother doing dishes just does not come into focus.

At age thirteen, in an attempt to please her, I spent the odd Saturday evening tidying up our kitchen. This aroused not pleasure but concern.

"I know you can clean the kitchen beautifully, and it's so sweet of you to do it," she told me. "But I would be so much happier if you would just come into the living room and read a book with the rest of us."

It took time for me to absorb the idea that I could get kudos from my mother by ignoring the clutter around me in order to develop an inner world. Eventually, I got behind the idea, and in the years since, no one I have lived with has accused me of being too tidy.

My mother's campaign to emancipate her daughter began, however, long before that. An important battle occurred at age six, when I requested — no, begged for — my first Barbie doll. To her, Barbie dolls were the handmaidens of evil, the ultimate enemy of womankind. And not only Barbies. Compromise requests for an "I Wet Myself!" doll would be stubbornly countered with educational specimens such as the stiff Spanish doll with the scratchy bouffant hairdo that I sullenly accepted one Chanukah. Tiny, unhuggable, ceramic dolls were presented after trips to Mexico. A box full of earnest little creations in native outfits lived in my bedroom closet. These dolls were "good for me", but I craved the trashy products of American pop culture. I did not care if they were subverting the struggle for women's equality, that they represented shallow, consumerist values. I wanted one.

By a stroke of outrageous fortune, my pathological need for a Barbie doll was finally answered with the help of a kindly *As It Happens* listener. This wonderful woman — whoever she was — sent as a gift to my mother an extraordinary collection of hand-sewn Barbie clothes, worthy of the House of Chanel. I don't know what possessed this woman to make so many gorgeous doll clothes and then give them to my mother. But because of this saintly person, I got not only a cherished Barbie (my mother was stuck — it was the only doll that could fit the clothing), but had the best-dressed Barbie in Canada. A satisfying conclusion to our struggle.

Eventually, I came to appreciate how fortunate I was that my parents took me as seriously as they did their sons. I felt lucky — even if the price of living so close to such a remarkable mother was that this friend of my youth, to borrow Alice Munro's beautiful phrase, was often not there.

My mother once said to a reporter: "I can tell you that my kids are not very impressed with me. They just think I'm their mother." But she was wrong. We knew that when she was not listening to us she was talking to Indira Gandhi about Punjabi independence, or Pierre Trudeau about wage and price controls, or Paul McCartney about wild times with the Beatles. We were impressed; and it soothed us.

There were constant reminders, both subtle and unsubtle, that our mother was special. When other kids' moms pulled out their best stationery to write excuses for absences from school, our mother scrawled her notes on grungy scrap-paper, or the backs of envelopes. These unsightly slips would be handed over with embarrassment by us, but would be snapped up with eager curiosity by our teachers.

Visiting her at the studio, I would think, Thank goodness my mother works someplace interesting because it would be boring to have to wait around for her in just an ordinary office. It didn't occur to me that if she worked in an ordinary office, I wouldn't be waiting.

Story editors would rush into the control room, "Here's the new cut, I hope it's the right length!" The director would bark at my mother, "Barbara, wrap this up, Beijing's waiting." The technician would manipulate a console containing, it seemed, thousands of buttons while rocking back and forth in his squeaky armchair. Despite my impatience to hear my favourite sound — that of theme music rising up over my mother's voice as she signed off, which was my cue that *now* we could go for dinner — pride would swell over me like a balloon at an old-fashioned country fair.

I remember a conversation with her from many years ago. I must have been just entering puberty. We were swimming together, and I was trying to persuade her that sometimes it was tough having an accomplished, prominent mother like her.

"I'll make you a deal," she said. "If you promise not to envy me, I'll promise not to envy you."

"Some deal," I remarked. "Why on earth would you envy me?"

"Lots of reasons," she explained. "Your youth could be reason enough but there's more. You have many gifts that I do not." A generous explanation, if she actually believed it. But she seldom said anything she didn't believe.

She trusted me like a friend and she made me her peer. "Dear Linny," she wrote to me when I was fourteen:

Tomorrow is my last day of work. The last week especially has been pretty hard and I'm looking forward to at least a week of thawing out before I'll feel normal again. Some days I feel if one more person tries to get me talking I'll fall apart. I crave silence very much lately. Talking for a living turns out to have its downside. Today Ron the technician wanted to read the newspaper out loud to me, Helen the secretary wanted to discuss her summer-kid-problems, Patty the story editor wanted to read a book at me to explain a simple item we had to do. Colin dropped by to find out why I hadn't signed my contract yet — on and on. A week in a monastery would feel very relaxing for the moment.

My mother had been taught by her mother to be independent on principle. That must have required immense self-restraint, because Florence was around all the time to monitor how my mother's independence was coming along. To achieve a slightly different result — independence for both child and mother — my mother had to rely on trust, respect, a great deal of luck, and faith that we would like each other at the end of the process. For all the inevitable difficulties, it was a wonderful way to be brought up.

In writing of my mother as a parent, I have been limiting the discussion to my elder brother David and myself. But I have another brother too. Matthew was born in November 1967, to a Native Canadian mother, and was adopted by our parents in June, 1968.

According to family lore, the decision to adopt Matthew occurred one evening, when I was five and David seven. The four of us were gathered in the living room, each privately engrossed in some book or game. Unhinged by the calm of it all, my mother turned to my father and said, "it's too quiet around here."

There is grim irony in this story for us because Matthew, more than solving the problem of "too much quiet", created a considerable upheaval. My mother was thirty when Matthew came to our home. She could have given birth to another child had she wished. But her angry sense of the injustices dealt the Native Canadians and — to use her words, her "bleeding liberal heart" — convinced her that the way to expand our family was through adoption. My father acceded to her wishes. As an only child he agreed, the more kids the better. How my mother accomplished that was up to her.

My mother expressed her concern over the status of Native Canadians in a *Chatelaine* article she wrote five months after Matthew's adoption:

> The Indians of Canada are a conquered people. Force this
> fact up out of your subliminal into your conscious mind
> and you will be ready to grasp what four hundred years of
> Indian policy have been all about. We've ghettoized Indian
> people on special lands not of their own choosing, forced
> Indian religion underground, outlawed the speaking of
> native languages in Indian schools, attacked Indian culture,
> overruled honourable treaties in our courts of law. History
> books written for white schoolchildren — and incidentally
> the only written sources available for Indian schoolchildren
> as well — perpetuate the concept of the noble savage, not
> so subtly implying that the half million Indian people now
> living in Canada are vestiges of a lost race... Canadians
> have no access to adequate, regular information about
> Indian history, values, music, religion or lifestyle to
> challenge the Hollywood-conceived image of the scalp-
> ing marauder.

Only later would my mother acknowledge the lapse in logic. She could not "save" a Native Canadian child by removing him from his culture and raising him in a white home. For a woman normally so analytical, so self-aware, she gave surprisingly little thought to the implications of interracial adoption. She was not alone in this. The wisdom of the day was that children and cultures could be mixed and matched in any combination — all you needed was love. She was struggling with two contradictory impulses: A desire to "rescue" a member of an oppressed group, and give him the chance of a better life, and the desire to honour his culture and origins.

These two impulses battled within my parents throughout Matthew's childhood. On the one hand they wanted to treat him exactly as they treated David and me...private schools, piano lessons, Hebrew lessons, Sunday school, and coaching him for a Bar Mitzvah. But when he showed neither interest nor aptitude, and often rebelled aggressively, they guiltily changed direction. They emphasized his physical education and exposed him to Native Canadian culture. But by acknowledging his differences, they were enhancing his alienation.

Many families have been torn by disastrous adoptions, and each is a special case, though there are grounds to speculate on some common causes. We have a greater appreciation today of the importance of bonding between a mother and her baby. Matthew came to us at seven months old, after three foster homes. We cannot guess about his natural mother's moods and conduct when she was pregnant with him, and whether this had an effect within the womb. What we know about heredity comes to us darkly; but we can see that for the child raised in the home of the parents who conceived it, heredity and environment reinforce one another in an irresistible mesh. For the adopted child, the two may work at cross-purposes; even when the child does not know it is adopted, perhaps it senses that it is not at home; perhaps, by heredity, the child reads the signals of the adoptive mother in a different way, and this mother and child can never entirely understand one another. Of course, the new parents might also be cruel, but this was emphatically not the case in our household; my parents loved Matthew.

My mother at first believed that unreserved love and affection could undo whatever damage a baby had suffered in his early months. But she did not believe that for long. Matthew, whom my mother received dirty and unwashed from his foster mother, squirmed away when she tried to hug and kiss him. He never enjoyed cuddling. He never hugged or kissed others.

Matthew was never truly happy in our home, although at times he could be so charming that you could easily convince yourself otherwise. At age two, he made his first poignant attempt to run away. I picture him as a child, always playing at the edges of our yard, looking outward, away. As he grew older he was more and more alone.

Several times my mother came home from *As It Happens* or *The Journal* to be confronted by a pair of policemen, explaining with sympathy and almost with embarrassment, that Matthew had been picked up for some misdemeanour. She loyally stood by him. Later, as the offenses grew more serious, the police stopped coming to the house, and summoned my parents to the station instead. They would stoically retrieve Matthew — or not, when they thought that might work better.

Since I was at McGill during the worst of these episodes, I missed much of the trauma. I did get a taste of it, however, when, only a few years ago, I went to a police station to report a missing wallet. When I gave the police officer my name, he nodded his head in recognition, as people do. I waited for the inevitable, "Any relation to Barbara?" but heard instead, "You mean, as in Matthew?"

My mother's generosity and kindness were tested. She discovered that she had large reserves of both. My father, who is genetically incapable of taking anything badly, explained to her, as well as to David and me, that this was Matthew's gift to us. He challenged us and taught us about our own weaknesses. Through Matthew we learned that good intentions are not enough.

I am sure that thought inspired my mother to write this prayer for Matthew at his Bar Mitzvah in November 1980.

God has set each of us in the midst of purposes we cannot measure nor understand. And yet we thank Him: For smiling

days like this; the life we have; for health, and healing;
earth and sky; for those thoughts of truth and justice which
move us to acts of goodness; and for the contemplation of
His eternal presence which makes us hope that what is good
and lovely cannot perish. Each one of us has burdens...
unique sources of pain, anxiety, sometimes despair...great,
aching gaps we yearn to close but never can. But each of
us has great gifts as well. Our prayer is that Matthew will
understand the very special blessings that grace his life.
And that he will use his great and marvelous talents to
build a life that blesses others, and in so doing, find
in return... respect, dignity, and a never-ending flow
of love.

My mother gave as much as she could to Matthew, and when
she had satisfied herself that there was no more she could do, she
withdrew for her own self-preservation. While he lived under her
roof, Matthew never became the straight arrow my mother had
hoped for. As June Callwood says, "She said to herself about
Matthew: maybe we made a million mistakes, but we loved him, we
did our best, we tried everything, and it's now up to him. It will
work or it won't."

Soon after his Bar Mitzvah, in a last-ditch effort, my parents
sent Matthew to Elan, a school in Maine offering "tough love" psychological counseling. They sent him this letter in anguish.

Dear Matthew,

We write these thoughts on the plane home from Elan,
trying to sort out our feelings about what lies ahead. And this
is the conclusion we've come to, Matthew.

We love you. We want you to be a full member of our
family. We want more than anything to see you happy with

yourself and with the world. We want you to be a solid citizen who likes himself because he knows he's a decent and productive member of society. You've pushed us to the limits and beyond as far as we are going to go. Now we're finished unless you change. We've come to the end of the road of begging you to get your act together. We aren't prepared to take any more blame because you think it's our fault that you're unhappy. Every problem is always somebody else's fault. Never Matthew's. We don't think we've done one single thing terrible to you that would justify your anger against us.

Every kid has got beefs with his parents and with the world — us included; David and Linda included. Of course we aren't perfect — we never pretended we were. But what on earth have we ever done to you to explain the grief you've been dishing out to us?

The harder we tried to convince you that you could succeed, the more you laid back and let us do all the sweating. The more we helped you (beginning with [your tutor] Mrs. Brown so you could pass Grade 2 & 3 & 4; then [the after-school program] T.L.C. when Harrison Rd. wouldn't put up with you anymore; then Crescent and your Bar Mitzvah, then convincing Lake Rosseau School you were a wonderful guy who deserved another chance) the more you lied to us, played games with us, stole from us.

The more we went through hoops to make you like yourself enough to start caring about other people, the more irresponsible and indifferent to everybody else you became. And how does making fools of us do anything good for you?

It's time to grow up, Matthew, time to give and not just take. You are at Elan to change your behaviour and to figure out how to stop feeling so miserable, so selfish, and so sorry for yourself. Every member of this family has to be a good and decent person who works hard and helps the rest.

If you come home it can only be as a person who cares about others and not just himself. No more mean old us, poor innocent you.

If you decide to get your behavior in order, we'll be the happiest two people in Toronto. We love you and we hate to see one of the luckiest guys who ever lived blowing his life away.

But it's up to you now, Matthew. We've reached our limits. You can't expect anybody, not even us to keep giving and giving, forgiving and starting again and again if you don't feel one drop of anything for anybody but yourself.

We pray you decide to grab hold and get your life straightened out, but now, Matthew, it's up to you.

My father added in his handwriting:

This letter was written by Mum because she has much the clearer handwriting, but the message is mine as much as hers. All the thoughts and hopes in this letter we worked out together. We are together in demanding that you get your act together. As we said, it is up to you! Our hopes and thoughts are with you.

Mum and Murr

After Elan, though not because of it, Matthew did change, in a positive direction. In the years before my mother's death he moved to Vancouver, where with her encouragement he began exploring his Native Canadian roots. Recently he was reunited with his birth mother, and separately with his birth father. He now has relationships with each of them as well as with several half siblings.

He continues to be in contact with my father, who gives him support and love. But to my mother, her failure with Matthew was a very great sorrow.

With David at his wedding, 1987

Chapter 10

Like Mother, Like Son

BARBARA FRUM:

Can I make a toast to our listeners — to the people who have kept us going for ten years?

BARNEY DANSON:

I'll drink to that. They're the same people who vote.

AS IT HAPPENS, *December 1978*
An interview with Canada's former defence minister

"To ME, Barbara Frum was the CBC." That sentiment, or some variation of it, was expressed in so many of the letters we received after my mother's death. My mother was proud to be the best-known face on the CBC. Unfortunately, the identification was so complete that viewers sometimes assumed she endorsed every word spoken on the network. My mother's involvement with a documentary on a civil war in some distant place might have been limited to reading a card that said, "Tonight on *The Journal*: the civil war in Remote-istan." But if the documentary championed North Remote-istan over South Remote-istan, my mother would sooner or later hear herself praised — or blamed — for her Northern sympathies.

Nothing bothered her more. My mother believed journalists could — and therefore should — forget their own opinions when reporting a story. So intensely did she subscribe to this old ideal of journalistic objectivity, that she would sometimes claim not to have any opinions at all. That wasn't true, of course. But it *was* almost an aspiration. And she was remarkably undogmatic and open to new evidence and new ideas. Her mind was constantly evolving.

My mother's belief in objectivity might have been unrealistic. Most of her colleagues in the media nowadays are sceptical that objectivity is either possible or desirable. Robert Fulford expresses well the view of most contemporary journalists: "I don't think you can be a human being and be present... without revealing a great deal of what you are thinking either through your voice or your face."

And maybe Fulford is right. But my mother managed to reveal less of herself than almost anyone else on television. I am often asked today, even by people who worked with her for a decade, what her political opinions really were. That would have pleased her. She deemed an interview a failure if a viewer could infer what her stance might be.

Perhaps she succeeded all too well. Her attempts to keep her opinions off the air made it too easy for her admirers to exalt her as the Conscience of Liberal Canada, and for her critics to condemn her as the Chief Propagandist for Canadian Socialism. (*The Journal* was often in the hands of fairly left-wing producers.) My mother's discretion has made it possible for amateur psychologists to misunderstand her relationship with my brother David, especially since her death.

It is one of the hard-to-believe coincidences of my life that I grew up not only with one of the country's most astute question-askers, but also one of the continent's most thoughtful answer-givers. In the past few years, my brother has become almost as well-known for arguing his views as my mother became by hiding hers. David's 1994 book *Dead Right* was hailed even by the unsympathetic *New York Times* as "the smartest book written from the inside about the American conservative movement," and by William F. Buckley Jr. as "the most refreshing ideological experience in a generation."

David began his journalistic career as a columnist for the *Yale Daily News* in 1980. He has published articles in virtually every important magazine and newspaper in Canada, the United States and Britain: the *Atlantic Monthly, Harper's, New York Times, Washington Post, Times Literary Supplement.* He worked for three years as an editor at the *Wall Street Journal,* and is now a contributing editor to the *Weekly Standard* in Washington, D.C. He broadcasts a weekly comment on *National Public Radio* and publishes a column every weekend in the *Financial Post* and *Toronto Sun.* I have sisterly pride, but I don't need it to understand his stature as a hugely influential conservative thinker on both sides of the U.S.– Canadian border.

What did my mother think of this? At a 1995 benefit in Toronto for PEN, a charity dedicated to protecting writers from persecution, comedienne Mary Walsh ventured a guess. "Speaking of torturing writers — what about David Frum? That little ingrate — I bet his poor mother is spinning in her grave."

Walsh's jibe prompted me to write a letter of protest. My family had contributed time and labour to the PEN benefit, and it seemed a rather shocking display of hypocrisy for the night's star attraction to joke that, come to think of it, she would like to see some writers tortured. But as for her charming crack about my mother, I had to shrug my shoulders. Unwilling to talk politics, my mother had never spoken candidly in public about her feelings towards David's ideas.

In fact, on the one occasion that she did talk to the press about

David, she was shockingly uncandid. In one of her last interviews, done just two months before her death, the *Globe and Mail* correspondent, Stephen Godfrey, asked her directly whether she was as right-wing as her son.

She replied, "When people call me right-wing, I think it's hilarious. I suppose they think that (way) because my son, David, is right-wing, which has made people question twenty years of my work. But we disagree about almost everything. If I thought people were serious in calling me right-wing, I would be hurt; I regard myself as a fifties small-l liberal. But people shouldn't know that from watching *The Journal*."

I was in Berlin visiting a friend when that interview appeared in the *Globe*. My mother was so upset about it, she tracked me down, and we spoke about it for an hour. As she explained to me from bed — the article had made her too depressed to rouse herself — what Godfrey had really wanted to talk about was her increasingly obvious illness. She was desperate to divert him. And so she made a trade: one taboo subject for another. "The day after the story appeared," David remembers, "she called me terribly upset to apologize. She said she had done something cowardly. She knew that Godfrey wanted to write a story about her illness, and to keep him away from that subject, she threw him a bone, something else he could make a story out of." Godfrey took the bone about her relationship with David, and broke the story of her illness too.

As Godfrey did not get near the complicated heart of my mother's political relationship with David, I will make an attempt.

The statement my mother made was half true. She was not "right-wing", at least not in her own mind. She thought of herself as a liberal, and called herself one. But she certainly didn't disagree with David about virtually everything. In fact, one of David's favourite jokes has long been to threaten to tell the world how much they *did* agree.

From his earliest childhood, my parents recognized gifts in David, just as Florence and Harold had recognized them in my mother. And my mother raised David the way Florence had raised her: "like a prize plant" as David now quips. Did Florence raise her daughter to be a debating partner? That's how Barbara raised her son.

Childhood family trips were arranged around David's interests. When a ten-year-old David memorized the roll call of the Roman emperors, my father announced a three-week family trip to Italy. (My father still tells the story of bringing David up to the gate for his first glimpse of the Roman Forum, to be crushingly disappointed when David politely said, "It's very nice." Until then, nobody had realized that David is severely near-sighted. My father quickly and accurately deduced that blindness could be the only possible explanation for David's response.)

Years before those trips, David had laid his hands on my mother's college history textbooks. He read them over and over again, beyond memorization to the threshold of understanding. And then on. John Macfarlane, the editor of *Toronto Life*, has written, "The first time I met David Frum, he was reading Will and Ariel Durant's *History of Civilization*. He was eight years old."

As David turned his mind to politics in his early teens, he naturally absorbed my parents' views, as they then were. "Before I developed ideas of my own," David says, "I became good at articulating my parents' ideas." He read the magazines that came into our house: the sharply left-wing *Canadian Dimension*, *Last Post*, *Village Voice* and *(More)*. In the early seventies, the *Atlantic* and *Harper's* were the most conservative periodicals in our mailbox; my parents had given up both *Commentary* and the *Public Interest* when those publications turned to the right after 1970. When fourteen-year-old David wanted to work on a political campaign, my parents signed him up with one of the candidates in the 1975 Ontario provincial election — a New Democrat. But David changed. And my mother — and all of us — changed with him.

"To an almost embarrassing degree," confesses my once politically liberal uncle Gerry, "David has influenced everyone in the family. I don't think that is because he set out to convert us. If anything, I think people tried to talk David out of his somewhat unorthodox views and in the process of arguing things through, the result was that more people came around to David's thinking, than that anyone changed David's mind. When I say 'anyone' I guess I'm talking about Barbara and Murray and Florence and me."

The first way that David changed was by becoming an educational conservative. Although my mother had been the product of a school system in which discipline was kept, as a young mother in the sixties she was seized by the mania to eschew structure. She turned against schools like those that educated her. In 1967, she did a series on education for the *Toronto Star* which highlighted two schools, one traditional, the other one of the progressive schools that sprouted amid the flower culture. She sharply condemned the traditional school.

"The children have a reined-in, polite air. ... Teachers instructed by groups rather than by individuals. You will find an entire class copying off the blackboard the names of the provinces and their capitals, a whole class using its weekly art period to make identical caterpillars." At the progressive school, by happy contrast, "the class feels like a workroom rather than a classroom ... children are allowed to chew gum in class ... [the teacher] is barely noticeable in the room ... there's no formal recess for the students. They can go out at 9:50 or 11:40 if that suits them."

Fifteen years later, when my mother was meeting adult Canadians who did not know the names of the provincial capitals, she reconsidered her early enthusiasm. But as late as the mid-seventies, David and I were sent to a new junior high school that had been built literally without classroom walls. The few walls needed to hold the building up were painted purple and lime green, by way of apology.

My parents soon noticed that something was wrong. Looking back on it now, David diagnoses the trouble. "I was starving — starving for knowledge." Swallowing their distaste for educational traditionalism — and for private schools — my parents enrolled David in UTS (University of Toronto Schools) a very academic high school downtown. He loved it: he studied Greek and Latin, read Chaucer, and was elected school captain in his senior year.

Then it was my turn. I had reached tenth grade unable to spell or solve simple arithmetical problems. I was pulled by my ears to Havergal College, a school that exemplified the old-fashioned ways at which my mother had once scoffed. I loved it too.

David went from UTS to Yale. It was Yale — that citadel of ivy-league liberalism, that has been galvanizing young conservatives at least since William F. Buckley Jr. — that turned him right. And, ironically, it was my mother's teaching that was largely responsible.

When we were very little, my mother would tape-record mock interviews with us. One, taped when David was about eight, concerned his elementary school's practice of sending report cards home in sealed envelopes. "Do you think it's decent to treat a child as a non-person like that?" my mother demanded. "No," my brother said uncertainly — at which point the tape is interrupted by my father's voice. "What kind of instruction are you giving him in insurrection?" Years later, when David decided that something was wrong with liberals who couldn't muster the resolve to face down communism, or inflation, or moral decay, the insurrectionary lessons were remembered. She had taught him to be aloof with conventional opinion; to trust his own mind, and never be afraid of standing alone. She had taught him to be brave, and she had taught him the ethic of public responsibility that she lived by.

"She thought that the point of privilege was fearlessness," David says. "If you don't have to worry about being fired, what excuse can you have for not speaking your mind freely?"

Which is what he began to do. At Yale he thought his way out of the liberalism in which he'd been raised. He read the classics of conservative thought. He formed friendships with conservative students and professors. He came home on holidays brimming with evangelical zeal. And he found in my mother as receptive an audience as he found in all of us.

"The crucial difference between David and everybody in the family before David got to work on it," says Gerry, "was that we were liberal in that we put an enormous value on tolerance and treating respectfully other people's views even when we didn't think they were right. If I were to pick one idea of David's that most changed my view of the world, it was his realization that we've systematically given people too much credit for good intentions when the obvious consequences of their actions are negative. I got that from a piece David wrote when Tommy Douglas died.

"Barbara had great empathy for anybody's suffering. But I think that what happened to her, and it would have happened with or without David, was that she came to realize the activists were making things worse, not better. While she had great empathy, she was never a sentimentalist. She wasn't willing to pretend that some government program was doing some good when it demonstrably was not.

"Did she learn this from David? I think it's just as plausible to say that David learned this from her."

By the late seventies, my mother had become nearly as Trudeauphobic as any Alberta redneck. She and my father had been caught up in the excitement of Trudeaumania in 1968, although they voted Conservative in that election because their friend Dalton Camp was the candidate in their riding. But the War Measures Act of 1970 and the prime minister's arrogant style permanently alienated them both. She feared that Trudeau would drive Quebec out of Confederation with his unyielding centralism, and the West away with his confiscatory economic policies. When David argued that what was bad for national unity was wrong on economic grounds too, my mother was disposed to listen.

"We had discussions around our dining-room table with the children ever since they could gurgle," says my father, another self-declared fifties liberal. "Their thoughts were always treated seriously. Over the years what I found was that winning arguments with David was always difficult because he didn't play fair. Because of his voracious reading and retentive mind, he could always marshal facts to support his opinion when much of the time, what I was dealing with was feelings."

My father is too modest. He is as shrewd and as knowledgeable a debater as David. And his political evolution — shaped by David but also by his encounters with government intervention and bureaucracy, had an effect on my mother's thinking too. Mark Starowicz bemoaned the influence of my father on my mother's economic thinking.

"To tell you the truth any time we did an economics interview the worst thing that could happen is that she would call Murray," Starowicz told me. "We would just get her briefed for this interview with the finance minister or something, and Barbara could get a bee in her bonnet about some clause or something, and we'd say frankly Barbara this is an eight minute interview. We're not going to get to that clause. And then she would talk to Murray and Murray would say, 'this is a shit budget,' or, 'the key thing about this budget is...' and that was it. We were lost. Whatever Murray thought about the budget became the core of the interview and that's God's living truth. It got to the stage, I confess, that when we were doing an economics story we would say, is there any way we can keep Murray busy? Because if she gets to Murray we've lost this one."

(When I told my father this anecdote he laughed and said, "that's not quite the way it was. Barbara would never rely on a single source, not even me. What she did was call her network of academics and business economists and then she formulated a line of questioning using me as a sounding board.")

Our mother was not "highly interested in economics," says David. "But she did care that Canada be a modern prosperous country. In the seventies, she was sold on the idea that the way to modernity and prosperity was to exclude foreign investment. But as it became clear that protectionism was the way — not to being modern — but to becoming Burma, and that it would also split the country, she turned her back on it."

From her speech to the graduating class of Brock University in 1987:

> The issues we face today have rarely been more complicated. Canada is making — because it must make — some definitive changes in how it manages its affairs.
>
> And while nothing is truly irreversible, these decisions — on trade, the constitutional arrangements by which we will be governed, tax reform, universality of social spending, the development of the third world — these are very close.
>
> We have dreamt we lived in Nirvana, we have been cocooned, cushioned, insulated from the traumas of the world, our neighbours are friendly, our political system is stable, we are relatively wealthy, we have enough to eat. We have a placid population not given to volatility or excess. Yet even we face profound wrenches as technology makes our natural inheritance less valuable and even feistier competitors look to their needs and wants in global terms.

The old certainties are far from certain. And the issues not as easy as the activists would have you believe. The new answers are to come not from the old, worn-out, visceral reactions. We need citizens to re-think and re-evaluate Canada's role in the world.

As with her views on feminism, her economic ideas evolved.

Through the eighties, the intellectual traffic between my mother and David grew thicker and thicker. There were arguments, of course. In some families, political arguments are proxies for other, more personal issues. Not in ours: my mother so enjoyed a personal discussion that if she caught the faintest whiff of underside, she would pounce on it with her trademark phrase, "Let's talk about what we're really talking about."

Perhaps the best test of what my mother thought of David was her insistence that he return to Canada after college (which he would not do at that time). It wasn't that she thought Canada would be good for David; she thought David would be good for Canada.

My mother's most passionate political commitment was to national unity. By the eighties, she had moved miles away from the Trudeau vision of Canada. She disliked the man, and she distrusted the journalistic impulse to make excuses for him. She distinguished herself as one of the few journalists willing to listen to what the Mulroney government had to say. One of the interviews where she failed her objectivity test, where the viewer could — as Robert Fulford described — see her real feelings, was the interview conducted with Brian Mulroney the day after the collapse of the Meech Lake Agreement. She prodded him to reveal the private, reflective side that he mysteriously withheld from the public. He resisted, becoming ever stiffer and more "prime ministerial" the more she pushed him to speak from the heart.

BARBARA FRUM:

Let me end on a personal note, if I could, and I don't know if you'll ever answer anything from the bottom of your heart and how you really suffered throughout this. But people saw your face and you looked pretty grim, pretty dispirited. A politician who puts this many eggs in one basket and suffers this kind of defeat, is thwarted in this way, what did that do to you?

BRIAN MULRONEY:

Well it . . . it was extremely unpleasant because my thoughts, Barbara, were really for the young people of Canada, for the children of Canada. I indicated to you earlier that I never thought of Meech Lake as a miracle. I thought of it as a bridge over which young English- and French-speaking Canadians could, over the next ten, fifteen or twenty years, know each other better and define a better country. But it would keep the country together so that our children could do perhaps a better job at it than we did. And I was profoundly dismayed when I saw such a modest initiative, but of such great importance, shot down for no reason and Canada being deprived of this very important instrument at a crucial time in our history. And so, on a personal basis, Barbara, I was very saddened by it, but as prime minister I know that the country can grow and can prosper and that we can find new ways of redefining a new Canada that, as I say, hopefully will continue to bring honour to all of us.

BARBARA FRUM:

How much responsibility do you put upon yourself for what happened here?

BRIAN MULRONEY:

Oh, I think that if you're prime minister of Canada at any

moment of difficulty the prime minister has to accept the responsibility and I do that.

BARBARA FRUM:

But to actually blame yourself for the failure, to see things that you did wrong?

BRIAN MULRONEY:

Oh, this is not an easy business. This is not... when you're trying to bring ten... I want to tell you that if you're trying to get ten provincial premiers in a room to get them to agree on something and we did it twice — twice I had their signatures on a piece of paper, unanimously and to see it go from that unanimous expression of unanimity and joy and confidence in Canada to a breakdown was a matter of great sadness and great disappointment to me, obviously.

Perhaps my mother's intellectual life could be thought of as a great arc, that in the end brought her back to the conservative liberalism of her Niagara Falls upbringing. That was the account she made of herself, and of her generation at the 1989 graduation ceremony at Simon Fraser University.

We were an unradical generation too we graduates of the fifties — seemingly eclipsed by our predecessors, who had fought and won a great world war and been so noble and self-sacrificing. And almost immediately eclipsed for sure by the radicalized students who followed right after us — mocked then and to this day — just read contemporary history books — as smug, uptight, materialistic, complacent, disgustingly middle-class and middle brow.

To the end my mother and David continued to disagree about many things. Seldom did they disagree about primary values. "People really misunderstood Barbara in thinking that her views were so terribly different from David's," says Gerry. "The most obvious point they had in common, it seems to me, is all of that which David calls 'the bourgeois values'. David and Barbara always thought alike on the subjects of personal responsibility, thrift, sexual prudishness. Those were constants. There was never any change in either of them on that score."

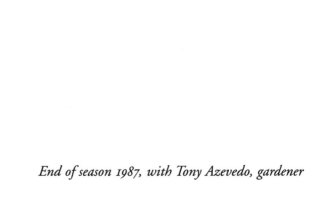

End of season 1987, with Tony Azevedo, gardener

Chapter 11

Points of Contact

God does most of it. I'm just tidying up.

BARBARA FRUM *in an address to a gardening society*

WHEN, AFTER HER DEATH, I asked George Jonas what he thought was the key to my mother's success as a journalist, he told me not to underestimate the importance of her skills as a chatelaine. Jonas, a writer who was a CBC producer when my mother's career began, suggested that she had thrown great dinner parties for the right people at the outset, and this had helped enormously to advance her career. When I asked Peter Gzowski, whom she first met at a dinner party, if he agreed with this somewhat cynical theory, Gzowski said, "The point is, it is the same skill that makes you good at both."

My mother definitely inherited her mother's flair for entertaining. Whether it was small, sumptuous dinner parties or loud, large garden parties, the frequent hosting of old and new friends was part of my parents' lives from the beginning of their marriage. Real friends were invited, never my parents' professional acquaintances — if that's all they were. They avoided getting bogged down in "duty" invitations. It is probably true that by socializing with important and prominent people, especially media figures, my mother raised her status and opened opportunities to herself. But she enjoyed entertaining for its own sake, as an outlet, as stimulation, as fun; and, in her later years, as a source of distraction and merriment when nothing else could lift her spirits.

As a hostess she skilfully drew out her guests and raised interesting topics of conversation. She could always be relied on to have something fresh to say. She loved to cook, and prepare inventive meals.

During her *As It Happens* years, when she could arrange her Friday schedule so as to be home by 7:30 (the rest of the week it was closer to 9:00) she and my father would have dinner parties almost every Friday. There was a period during my adolescence when I felt as if I held down a part-time waitressing job. As the famous Canadian hostess Sondra Gotlieb once said to me, "In the seventies, people thought it was charming if their kids did the serving, even when the prime minister of Canada came for dinner."

There was a system to the dinner parties of this time. During the day, our housekeeper of the moment would cook festively according to my mother's instructions. Arriving at the house at the same time as her guests, my mother would breeze in the front door and oversee the final details; mixing the sauce just so, choosing the appropriate silver platters, removing dessert — invariably a meringue and ice cream dish — from the freezer. All the rest would fall to me: serving food, refilling wine glasses, clearing dishes, fetching ashtrays.

One formative experience of my youth was watching my parents make seating assignments the nights before their parties. It was painfully clear that there were desirable seating companions, and undesirable. The undesirables, I noted with internal alarm, were almost always women. This was still the era of "wife of" and my parents would hold certain name cards in their hands and say wearily, "Who gets her?" If there was ever a motivation to do something with my life it was this.

One of the most withering comments I remember my mother uttering was after a dinner party when a bachelor friend had brought a new, decorative date. "She was lovely," I remember my mother saying the next day, "but she had nothing, you know... *helpful* to say. She insisted on giving her opinions on the Constitution but they just weren't... *helpful.*"

Sometime in the mid-seventies, my parents, along with a group of their closest friends initiated an annual New Year's party. These elaborate pot-luck dinners were usually held at my parents' house for a few reasons, the size of their kitchen among them, but also because having it at home meant that David and I could attend too. "I think there is some resentment that our kids get to come," my mother warned us conspiratorially one year, "so don't be too intrusive." We were so accustomed to being treated by our parents as intellectual equals (my mother had, after all, once explained that she thought of us as "people who happen to live under the same roof"), it was easy to forget that their friends could hold a different view.

"You children were there more often than other people's children," says Robert Fulford, who with his wife Geraldine were my parent's most frequent dinner guests. "Florence too. One way or another, Florence has met most of Barbara's friends. They all had opinions on her, reacted to her. Barbara was inclusive. You would see a lot more of the Frums *en famille* than you will of most families." Delicately put.

By 1983, the guest list for the New Year's party had grown so large that it had to be held in a party room at a Toronto restaurant. The raucous flavour of the event is conveyed in this thank-you letter from Michael Enright, later to become a host of *As It Happens*:

Barbara:

   Murray atop a table is one of those rare sights, like sunset in the Vale of Kashmir or Ronald Reagan reading a book, that one has to cherish for years. Speaking on behalf of the new-comers, I'd just like to say the entire evening was a delight. And I think those four people in the other room would agree. As a modest token of our appreciation, I will be contacting the other newcomers over the next few days with a view to buying Murray a set of Dolores del Rio castanets for next year. Have a happy new year.

When she hosted *As It Happens*, my mother was famous for her laugh, a sometimes throaty, sometimes soft, easily provoked bit of music. It was always one of the great mysteries of our family life that although my mother loved to laugh she was incapable of telling a joke. Not only did she never tell jokes, she often missed them. Our whole family might be doubled over in hysterics about some-thing someone had said and my mother would sit perplexed, ask-ing impatiently, "What's so funny? I don't get it!" Someone would explain the joke and then she would smile in a good-natured sort of way and say, "Oh, I see. Yes, that *is* funny." It was clear she still didn't get it. Eventually we realized that she took almost everything literally. Precisely the quality that made her a great interviewer — the insistence on exactness — cut her off from forms of humour that hinged on ambiguity, sarcasm and double-entendre.

During her *Journal* years, my mother's penchant for entertain-ing waned. Even on special occasions, such as a birthday or anniver-sary, my mother could not dream of getting out of the studio before 9:40. Friends could be entertained only on weekends, but since there was so much my mother had to pack into them, she was pleased to dine alone with my father. Her time with him became increasingly precious. Even with a full table of guests, dialogue with my father maintained its primacy. My mother would often unself-consciously interrupt guests, even those in anecdotal mid-flight, to coo, "Murr...This chicken is barbecued to perfection! You've outdone yourself." Or, if she had been the cook, "Murr, you have to admit I've done a great job with the pasta." My father's response would be equally direct and exclusive.

I was always amused and somewhat embarrassed to watch guests deal with this breach of etiquette. Inevitably they would pause to agree that the barbecue or pasta was delicious and then innocently continue with the story. "Murr!" my mother would again interrupt, "what a wonderful wine you're treating us to tonight..."

With pity I would look at such guests and watch them flounder. I could see what they were thinking: Should they now praise the wine? Or push ahead with the story at accelerated speed in the hope of finishing it before the next interruption? Or just shut up and admit defeat? No matter which option they selected, they had to accept that, at any moment, my mother's attention would drift towards her husband, with no guarantee that it could ever be won back.

But more often my mother was gracious and the parties she and my father hosted are now fabled.

"If you want to know where the power is in Toronto, go to a Barbara Frum party," wrote Allan Fotheringham in 1989 after my mother and father hosted a glitzy party for William Thorsell to celebrate his appointment as editor of the *Globe and Mail,* adding: "Barbara is the den-mother-cum-traffic-cop among the town's personalities in broadcasting, journalism, the book industry, and the arts world in general."

"More than in most people's houses you felt that something important was going on," says Robert Fulford. "You felt that Barbara worked hard to make the event important. Although I never had the sense that you got there because you were famous. Their friends were not people who had all read the same book. [A well-known female journalist] said to me one time: 'We've met before. We met at the Frums. I was there as a date. I couldn't get there on my own.' I realized it was for her a place to get to."

My mother's love of entertaining and skill as a conversation-alist were always apparent to Fulford: "She obviously sparkled when a group of people came in. She was patient. She wanted other people to talk. She wanted to ask them questions, to find out what they were doing, what they were thinking about. She had an inter-viewer's tic — which is, even when she had a point of view she defended it with a question. About a movie that she hated and I loved, she would say, 'Well, Bob, what is so great about it?'"

At parties thrown by others, however, Fulford noticed more reticence. "At other people's houses and at cocktail parties — and she went to an awful lot — she quite often stood at the door. Some-times, outside the door. I remember a party at Knowlton Nash's, at their apartment, there was quite a long hall from the elevator, and there were other guests in the hall so that she was not the only one, and she had on a kind of fringy shawl which she was playing with, and I don't know that she ever came into the apartment."

My mother used to say that if she hadn't become a journalist, she probably would have become a prosecuting attorney. I think she would have become a general contractor.

Architect Brigitte Shim, who, along with her husband Howard Sutcliffe, did the last wave of renovations on my parent's home, said of my mother in her memorial tribute:

> Barbara loved the act of construction. Like a child she thrilled
> to the sound of bulldozers and concrete trucks, the moving
> of earth and the sight of cranes. The re-locating of walls or
> mature trees, the reworking of hillsides or a suite of rooms
> were perfectly natural activities to her. . . . Three summers ago
> much of her vacation from *The Journal* was spent as a general
> contractor. Barbara . . . was out on the site at the crack of
> dawn every working day. She supervised the demolition of

Barbara Frum winning her fourth ACTRA award in 1980 — and still surprised.
Her mother, at the same table, is among those more purely delighted.

She became host of *The Journal* in 1981, and soon was a signature CBC TV
presence at political conventions, special events, and wherever the CBC's flag
was flying. But at home, she instinctively stood in the background.

Among my mother's closest friends and colleagues: Robert Fulford and Geraldine Sherman, Alan Wilkinson, Margaret Lyons, Sally Reardon, Max Allen, June Callwood, Mark Starowicz, Mary Lou Finlay, and Ruth Ellen Soles.

My mother and grandmother as pallbearers at Judy LaMarsh's funeral in 1980.

Interviewing the
world ... clockwise
from top right:
Nelson Mandela; a
child in the vicinity;
Hosni Mubarak;
Brian Mulroney;
Pierre Trudeau; and
Paul McCartney.

Barbara at home with the inevitable demi-tasse; my brother and I at his wedding; and a recent photo of my uncle Gerry with my father Murr.

The collecting mania was an organizing principle of my parents' life together.
In Tahiti; at home; and showing a reporter around the *African Majesty*
exhibition in 1981.

My mother went to great lengths to make her politics inscrutable to her viewers, so my brother David came as a surprise. Below, David and his wife Danielle, at their 1988 wedding in our mother's garden; their children, Miranda and Nathaniel.

Barbara with her double, Greg Malone of *Codco*. This autographed photo to him reads: "To my better half please pick on somebody else now." Below, another friendly barb, from Aislin.

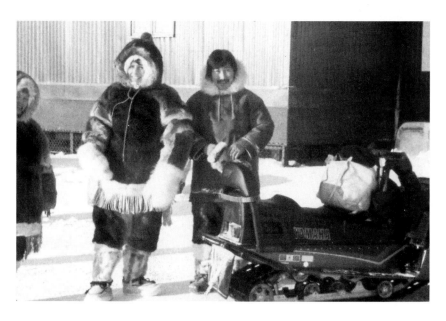

Making the rounds, this page, with Dasha and her father in their little apartment in Moscow; and on Baffin Island. Opposite page, receiving an honorary degree (at Simon Fraser); and at one of innumerable cocktail parties. Below, I speak to a non-existent audience in Regina. Mother told me there would be days like this.

One of the last photographs of my mother, in her dressing room with Diva standing guard as always. Celebrating *The Journal*'s tenth anniversary with Peter Mansbridge and Knowlton Nash: two months before Barbara's death, and eight months before *The Journal*'s.

Florence and my children, Samuel and Barbara.

an existing fence and construction of a new garden fence that was over 350 feet long. We often received early morning wake-up calls from Barbara, who had already been up, phoning lumber yards and comparing the prices for cedar two-by-eights and two-by-sixes.

My parents lived in the same house for thirty years, but it was never exactly the same. It changed constantly, sometimes in small ways, with furniture reassigned to different rooms, and sometimes dramatically with the construction of new wings, or a new water fountain, or the architecturally unconventional garden gazebo my mother affectionately dubbed her folly.

It's impossible to think of my parents' house as a single entity fixed in time. It is rather an amorphous collection of glass, wood, and brick sprawled across an acre of ravine-edged property which even now takes on new shapes and colours every year.

The builder's impulse in my mother, which lives on in my father, prevented them from having a house ever complete. Historians observe that Thomas Jefferson's home, Monticello, looks the way it does today only because Jefferson died before further renovations. In my mother's case, a large dumpster full of debris from the latest unfinished project had to be negotiated by friends calling on my father the morning after her death.

It is tempting to draw conclusions about my mother's psychological need to build as a way of making a contract with the future: "If I plan a new room," I can imagine my mother bargaining, "surely I can't be wiped away before it's done." Each of her renovations was an act of faith, but it is also true that the urge to build burned brightly inside her long before she knew she had cancer.

The decision to buy the one and only house my parents occupied for the duration of their marriage was made in their third year together, after David was born and my father's dental practice was established. Setting out on foot from their rented apartment on Elm Avenue, my mother searched the streets of Rosedale for the right home. Even at age twenty-four, she knew she was not looking for a version of the conservative "Georgian" house she had grown up in. Given her preferences, stately Rosedale was an odd neighbourhood to scout, and yet, on Park Road, not far from Yonge and Bloor, she found a house that made her pulse race. It was designed by the modernist Toronto architect James Murray, and owned by an elderly heiress to the Imperial Oil fortune. It was the closest thing to a Frank Lloyd Wright design in Toronto. With characteristic fearlessness, my mother knocked on the door to ask for a house tour. Since few would dream of house hunting in this manner, few would expect the following response: "The lady of the house has just died, but why don't you come in?"

Within weeks, my parents were locked in a fierce bidding war. They didn't get the house, but gained a clear view of how to proceed. My mother realized she would only be satisfied by building her own house. My father, the future real-estate developer, was hesitant. It seemed impractical and too expensive at their stage of life. But my mother was adamant. They narrowed their search to two plots of land: one in Rosedale and the other in suburban Willowdale. By chance, both lots would end up with houses designed by Ron Thom; my parents' was the one in Willowdale.

But ten years before Thom was contracted to renovate, my parents' first architect was a neighbour from the apartment building they had lived in as newlyweds. Yusing Cheung, who was also a friend from university, had never actually built a house before but that did not matter to my parents. "We were each full of ideas and we trusted him," my father remembers.

Every night Yusing and his wife would come over to my parents' apartment and the tracing paper would come out. "We talked about the philosophy of how to raise kids, and where the garden should be, and how the expansion should be planned," my father remembers. Built in 1963, the house was completed shortly after my birth.

"At that time Barbara was in tune with being a mother," my father says. "So we built a house where there were no stairs to go running up and down. You could take a toy train, and run it from one end of the house to the other without tripping over anything. It wasn't very big. There was a living/dining room and a scientifically designed kitchen with a window overlooking the courtyard so you could see where the kiddies were playing. It was really a house designed to raise kids in. The materials were tiles, nothing you could stain. The laundry was next to the kitchen. Barbara didn't want air conditioning, she liked the idea of feeling the hot nights, feeling the elements."

My parents lived happily in that child-centred home until 1972. Then, when we kids were older and my father had made the transition from dentist to developer, they were ready to build a residence more sophisticated and commodious. My mother described this transformation in the eulogy she delivered at Ron Thom's funeral in 1986:

> Shortly after Massey College was completed Murray called Ron on the telephone to ask if he would recommend to us someone who worked in his idiom to do a project for us. We loved Massey College — knew before the scaffolding came down that it was a masterpiece — and wanted to live in a house with that same spirit and serenity, though we were terribly timid about asking the genius architect who produced that marvel to do a mere house addition for us.
>
> The person Ron recommended was himself. And that was the beginning of a fifteen-year-long association, and friendship, in

which just about every spring Ron would be at our house where some new project was being entertained. Sometimes the project was as large as a room, sometimes as small as a table — we did the landscape together — we built the furniture together.

As he told us at that first meeting, he loved doing houses, enjoyed working closely with clients on the intimate sum of personal details that a house is.

Our kids soon learned it was truly spring, not when the robins arrived in the garden, but when Ron arrived at the front door — the buzz saws not far behind him.

Ron was an artist who made a refined aesthetic out of unrefinement, a master of the difference between complexity and fussiness. He taught us to love raw surfaces, and the natural, to recognize harmonious proportions, how good it is to sleep and eat close to the floor, to be wrapped at night in the cocoon of a dark room, punctuated by the sparkle of tiny beams of light, how everything went together if you only knew what you were doing — how many steps made a walk inviting, how many made a destination too far, and how broad the treads must be — which he'd dance out for us to teach the difference, striding up and down across the floor.

Ron loved solving riddles and we sometimes felt he built problems into his drawings so he could be summoned in desperation by anxious clients to dazzle them with the brilliance of his remedies.

Ron was never happier than when he could place some British Columbia mood down on a Toronto street —

sometimes with an excess of wishful thinking — which produced occasions like Murray's discovering that Ron's specs called for single glazing throughout the house against the Ontario furies; or the morning when Murray (who revered Ron's talent) called rather apologetically about two corners of the living room without any glazing called for at all and said that if that was Ron's intention, he, Murray, was prepared to try it for one winter, though he doubted it would work for two.

The big room he built for us remains to my mind one of the finest, most humane spaces he ever produced — an enormous, deceptively simple square, about which he slung an overhanging triangle with both levels cantilevered off an unornamented slab of caramel brick, the whole hunkered down under a shallow hill and married to the landscape through the mediation of a pair of suspended trellises. . . . His space is never austere, it's for human beings. And we have never had a visitor yet who didn't smile in recognition of the embracing comfort he envelopes you in, and didn't leave saying: "I'd love to live here."

Carping about my parents' love of renovation is a well-developed habit from my adolescence. David and I, not always good-naturedly, bemoaned the regular disruption of our lives.

To our taste, too many school mornings began with the blurting of sleepy salutations to the troop of carpenters who inhabited our kitchen — instead of our parents, who rose after we'd left for school. One carpenter in particular was a regular spring visitor. He became a friendly surrogate parent, asking us about our tests and homework as we climbed over tool boxes, heaps of nails, sawdust, and chain saws to place a slice of bread in a toaster.

Although as children we escaped the trauma of moving houses, I could become very grumpy watching the landmarks of my childhood — walls, rooms, windows — tumble one by one. You knew when you left home for the summer, that the house would not be the same when you returned. There was no telling whose personal space would be invaded. One summer I received a letter that announced:

> We've decided how to do your room. . . . We take out everything but the closet. Put the bed on a raised platform. Rebuild your drawers, and build a new and better desk. I hope you're pleased. You're a grown up young woman now and you need a better private space.

Another summer:

> I spent all day today getting into mischief when I should be lying under a tree reading a serious book. I went to Ginger's to look for a beige sink to replace the one that's scratched in our bathroom. Of course that takes a new counter top to hold the sink up — and if I'm already doing that, I hate those plastic taps. Will you scream if I buy a gold faucet? . . . Of course a kitchen store was on my list too. I'm not touching your room, don't worry.

And later the same summer:

> Murray says I've already got too much time on my hands — today I rented a floor sander and stripped the porch floor back to its original cedar colour, plus I took in the chaise longue pillows to be reupholstered in white vinyl — very Hollywood-glam — with brown piping.

Although these changes were generally improvements, children have strong conservative instincts, and my mother's efforts on my behalf would be greeted as often with outrage as with thanks.

Yet another of our parents' summer projects happened after we children had left home. The formica and tile "kids' bathroom" — once decorated with our parents' "Make Love Not War" posters — became a gold-fauceted sky-lit domed luxury pit, with a whirlpool tub in one corner and a tubular shower capsule in the other. Every surface in the room was covered with slabs of smoky-red marble, removed from Iran at the height of the Iraq–Iran war. Glancing at the finished product, my brother David remarked: "I feel like I'm visiting the Kuwait Hilton."

The renovation that was underway shortly before my mother's death involved merging my own with Matthew's former bedroom to make a large guest bedroom. This required the removal of childhood relics I had stubbornly left in place. I resisted her entreaties to remove my high school yearbooks, cultural dolls, and long-outgrown summer dresses. It gave me sentimental pleasure whenever I came home to see my youthful belongings just where I had left them.

But my mother insisted: "I can't store these things for you, Linda. My house is not a warehouse."

"But I have no room at my apartment!" I cried, which was arguably true. Really, I couldn't bear to see my childhood disassembled. "You have this huge house, what do you care?"

"Girlie!" my mother said with mock gravitas, "I need the space!"

Given all the additions over so many years, we both knew my mother was not short of space. "You're going to have to make tough decisions about what to keep and what to throw out," she explained. "I'm doing it too!"

It is eerie to me that this massive housecleaning was undertaken just months before my mother's death, though also months before I understood that her light was fading. It was as though *she* knew that she would soon be gone, and was organizing every room, closet, photo album and filing cabinet in anticipation. Although she gave no clue, she helped us all through a painful process while she was still here and well enough to do it. If her life was organized and full of consideration for others, so too were her home and her affairs when she died.

Over the decades, my parents' house had been transformed from tiny kid heaven, to an expansive home designed exclusively for Barbara and Murray. ("The world's largest one-bedroom apartment," David would tease.) It became a haven, a sanctuary, and an art gallery for the two lovers inhabiting it.

I mustn't be dismissive about my parent's need for gallery space. One of the greatest passions of their lives was an art collection of African tribal sculpture.

Psychoanalyst Werner Muensterberger in his book, *Collecting*, has called this habit in general "an obsession", "an addiction", an "unquenchable thirst", all of which phrases describe my parents at the height of their collecting mania. My mother told *Maclean's* magazine in 1981, the year the Art Gallery of Ontario mounted *African Majesty*, a major exhibition of their collection, that "I personally despise the word 'collector'. When you're passionately in love with something, you aren't in control." She also called her desire to collect, "A crazed compulsion like an illness."

This illness was provoked innocently enough by the random acquisition of an ancient Egyptian sculpture at New York's Metropolitan Museum in 1957. Married only two months at the time, my parents were in New York on a trip with Florence and Harold. Harold had recently indulged his own unruly passion for luxury cars, and had driven the four of them to New York in his new Lincoln. At the Metropolitan, they were surprised to find a showcase of Egyptian objects on display just inside the museum's front doors. The museum was in the process of "de-accessioning" (a practice frowned upon by the museum culture of today).

"The woman behind the counter was a curator and a Canadian besides," my father remembers. "She took us downstairs and showed us a huge room full of things for sale. I did not have the wit to buy the whole room. I should have gone into hock to buy everything. But we were little children and we didn't know about these things. The piece we bought was from the Middle Kingdom, 2500 B.C. It had been found on one of the Met's expeditions. It was a totally beautiful object: a walking priest made of wood. Remnants of paint were still visible. The price was seventy-five dollars — in today's dollars that's probably $750. It was totally crazy. Still, I didn't have seventy-five dollars. I had just bought my dental practice, and I was in debt. So we ran back to Harold who lent us the seventy-five dollars to buy the piece. To this day, I've never seen a better one. I've seen bigger but not better."

The purchase taught my parents that they both loved sculpture, and both loved wood. But they were not yet feverish. That took until the early seventies.

"We took a trip to Montreal," my father remembers, "and saw in the window of a shop what we thought was a Mayan mask. So we went in and asked about it. Now, there's no such thing as a Mayan mask but we didn't know that at the time. We just saw the coloring of it and thought it was reminiscent of a Mayan headdress. It was a painted wooden mask. As it turned out, it wasn't Mayan at all, but African. It was very beautiful and so we bought it."

It was an Ibo mask from Nigeria, which cost $650. The piece itself was not exceptional, but it caused the collision between two natural collectors and the art form they must collect. After flirtations with Egyptian, Mayan, and Canadian art, they had found something that answered to their calling.

"When we travelled we now started to look for African pieces," my father says. "We started to really like it, to read about it. When we first started buying it, what we discovered was that we could purchase pieces of tribal art of international importance, of museum quality, for relatively small sums of money. It happened to be a moment when there was a break-up of collections because of a generational thing. At that time, African was an out-of-fashion art form. It had been in high fashion in the twenties and thirties when the Cubists and Surrealists were highly sought and people could see the link. And many of the collectors in France had bought them in conjunction with paintings by Picasso, Braque and Modigliani. Then for some reason it went into decline during the forties and fifties. When we came at it, it was still in relative decline. It hadn't jumped the way most of the art market had."

My parents were pleased to collect something that was a mystery to most people. The obscurity of African art, at least during the seventies, allowed them to collect without the fear of appearing ostentatious, which they dreaded. It was almost like having a secret.

"My husband would clobber me if he read that I publicly announced what we've been spending on these pieces," my mother told *Medicine Hat News* when they did a feature on Canadians who collect. "Not that people really appreciate their value," she added. "Most people want to know why we have all that driftwood around the house."

Within a few years, our formerly stark house was crammed with ferocious nail fetishes, life-sized African kings, macabre bags of bones with ancestor relics, and warrior masks made, possibly, from human skin.

My parents' collection of driftwood soon became significant. "From a museum standpoint," says Michael Kan, curator of African art at the Detroit Institute of Art, and North America's leading African Art scholar, "it is without a doubt one of the finest collections of African Art in private hands."

Perhaps because they felt some embarrassment over the speed at which their collection grew (David and I were the prime witnesses) they tried to feign indifference.

"The auction books finally arrived and there's not one interesting thing for Murray to lose his heart (or wallet) on. Thank goodness," wrote my mother to my brother in 1976. Such statements were well-meaning but never true. What collector is ever without some new object of desire?

The tone of another letter to David was more realistic:

> You knew, of course, that Murr could not return home without another piece of rotting wood. But this time he has really outdone himself. In fact he may collapse from an attack right at the baggage pickup when this bruiser comes rolling down the ramp. I don't know what he thinks he's doing putting this in his luggage allotment. Plus there isn't a taxi in Toronto that would try to transport it. Oh, the scenes that lie ahead next week when our Bamileke king is brought to the airport to meet us for his trip to his new home. ... I must say though, Dave, you aren't missing a great trip. We aren't very energetic. The auctions were a bore.

It was extremely rare for my parents to return from one of their trips to Europe without a new piece of wood. But it was also extremely rare for them to acquire anything that they weren't both completely in love with. "Most collector husbands and wives have interminable arguments about things," says Kan, who often encountered my parents at auctions of tribal art in Paris and London. "But Barbara and Murray had this wonderful harmony together — it's the kind of thing people dream about. Usually with a collecting couple, there is quite a bit of surrender by one or the other. Barbara and Murray were both very strong, except in different ways. That was what was so interesting... there wasn't any locking of horns. At least not in front of me."

In his tribute to my mother at her memorial service, Alan Wilkinson, the Art Gallery of Ontario's distinguished former curator of modern sculpture, and a dear friend of our family, described their acquisition process:

> What I found so stimulating when we got together to discuss a possible new acquisition was the depth of the analysis, the comparisons with other works, the books and catalogues spread all over the dining-room table — Barbara thought the head was wonderful but the legs weak, whereas Murray admired the torso. Barbara often brought out her magnifying glass to "examine a crack of wood or to look for possible restoration.

However, Alan was also party to several occasions when my parents did not work together in exact harmony:

> At auction, Murray did the bidding, having agreed beforehand on the upper limit. On one occasion, however, I remember Barbara desperately trying to control Murray's hand which kept going up and up as did the price — far beyond the limit they had set! Another time Barbara took things into her own hands. Murray, having just bid successfully for a sculpture, left the room to pay for it. Upon his return, he was amazed and amused to find Barbara, completely out of character, enthusiastically bidding on something they hadn't even discussed.

> On a visit to Paris they were offered a rare Dogon Horse and Rider. Murray loved it. Even though the head of the horse was missing, the rider was elegant and regal. But Barbara wasn't convinced and this time vetoed the purchase. She

returned to the hotel for a nap. Murray slipped back to the dealer and bought the sculpture. When Barbara woke up and saw the headless horse, she muttered: "Look at that, leave Murray on his own for half an hour and he comes back with a horse's ass." Murray has assured me that the carving was to become one of her favourite works.

"A lot of collectors collect in very uniform fashion," says Kan. "It's almost predictable what they will go for. Murray and Barbara departed from that. There are two distinct areas in their collection: the polished, exquisite, classic, small things from the Congo and Gabon, and the Yoruba and Cameroon stuff which tends to be, in comparison, very violent and expressionistic. It certainly makes them different from other collectors. There are wide swings in their collection of period and culture. As I remember it, the Gabon Kotas were always sitting on a Louis XIV Boulle desk. You may see such an arrangement in the home of a Rothschild in Paris, but it is very unusual to see that in a home in Canada."

As Kan hints, my parents acquired much art in addition to their African collection including French furniture, Oceanic sculpture, Canadian and American modernist painting. In their kitchen hung a large, glass-framed, Andy Warhol portrait of Chairman Mao, visible through the window to every Chinese food delivery man, who would cringe as he handed us the bags. The display of this ghastly man was mitigated over the years, as my mother came to use Mao's face as a kind of bulletin board on which to tape shopping lists, photographs, phone messages, and interesting pieces of mail.

Of all her personal loves — entertaining, renovating, art collecting — none gave my mother the tactile, soul-soothing pleasure of her most cherished pastime: gardening. As with everything else, she seized upon it with ambition and zeal. "Gardening," she admitted, "is the perfect hobby for a compulsive personality."

She came to gardening late though she had always had a sensitive interest in her environment. In the early seventies, a townhouse development went up across the street from our home. My mother was offended by its aggressive ugliness — she referred to these houses as the "Roman Ruins", and railed against a society that would allow such blight in its sightlines.

Walking through the ravine behind our house, she would become outraged at the amount of litter. She called the two neighbouring high schools and in her most seductive voice explained to their principals, "This is Barbara Frum calling. I would like to come to your school to address your student body on a subject I know all young people today are deeply concerned about: the environment." The principals, delighted by this unsolicited act of apparent generosity, hastily agreed. My mother's address to the students was brief: "If this generation cares as much about the environment as you're always going on and on about, then *stop throwing ice-cream wrappers on my lawn!* Thank you."

The religious experience of a CBC promotional trip to Baffin Island — according to her, one of the most heart-stoppingly beautiful places on earth — was almost ruined when she discovered discarded orange peels scattered across the tundra. "If she saw a candy-bar wrapper on a beach it would touch off a whole lecture on human depravity," David remembers. "The human impulse to desecrate was to her one of the real human evils."

The impulse to beautify, however, was irresistible to her. To celebrate their twenty-fifth wedding anniversary, my father wanted to give my mother a wonderful present. "Name anything you would like," he told her. "Jewellery? A fur coat? A car?"

"What I would love, what I would *really* love," replied my mother, "is six workmen and a bulldozer."

Her wish was his command, and my mother began a massive landscaping project that sustained her for the rest of her life. She planted hundreds of exotic plants, shrubs, and flowers: tree peonies, dwarf Japanese maples. She shipped in a mature, sixteen-foot rhododendron from Vancouver, and a rare weeping white pine from Oregon. These precious specimens were laid into the ground with giant cranes which my mother expertly supervised. She told one of her contractors: "Break a window on the house before you break a single branch of that tree."

Every morning during summer vacations she would go out into her garden, which became more lush and exotic with each passing year, and, with Diva and the gardener Tony as her companions, spend eight hours pruning, weeding, and digging. The garden contained her spirit. She felt comfortable with dirt up to her elbows, and was not squeamish about slugs, worms, or mice. She tended to each of the thousands of plants in her garden with the concerned care of a loving mother. This love was evident to the jealous Diva, who, my mother accused, deliberately trampled and urinated over any plant she sensed my mother was especially fond of.

"My biggest sin as a gardener is I'm extremely impatient," she told the host of a Vancouver gardening show with more candour than the viewers may have realized. "Good gardeners tell me: 'You have to be patient. You have to be with the spirit of the plant, you have to start with this little pygmy and you must wait.' And I say, 'I don't have time to wait. I'm not going to live that long.'"

She saw her garden as the metaphor of her life, as she wrote in this essay for Hilary Westin and Nicole Eaton's 1989 book, *In a Canadian Garden*:

> I am a relative newcomer to gardening and so my garden, like my life, is a work in progress, with many unresolved patches awaiting creative inspiration. I had been the relaxed custodian of a fairly routine suburban backyard until the mania struck about five years ago. But what's been clear from the day I

decided the backyard should be a garden is that, all along, I was destined for this affliction.

Now that I'm an addict, a spade won't do. When I take on a garden project, it requires earth-moving equipment, tons of fresh soil, full-grown trees and bushes dropped in by crane.

I think of gardens as the place for the bold stroke, the indulgence of whim, with all the inherent risks of folly. I've made my own austere composition in brown and green. Above all, I care about the contour of the land, about vistas, and about the form and placement of plants. I prefer a bank of moss and thyme and river-washed pebbles to an immaculate bed of perfect tulips. Bark and foliage move me more than a smartly clipped hedge or a splendid perennial border. I love blooms and blossoms, of course, and fragrance is a precious bonus, but my main goal is a landscape that's beautiful in all seasons, in the rain, under snow, in the sodden mists of March and in the sweet, sad, lavender light of late November.

To look good all year, a garden needs great bones. In my garden the structure comes from an undulating shallow valley with pine trees along its length, and from some creaky but elegant old black locusts which put out a frothy canopy of fronds each summer that dapples light down onto the woodland floor below.

It's my belief that the gardener is invariably a relentless, obsessive perfectionist, forever on the move across the landscape in a bent-over posture. Your visitor sees beauty and showers praise and encouragement. You see only mistakes to be corrected which, of course, is precisely what keeps you hooked.

Gardening for me is not about success or about contentment. It's about our struggle against time, about anticipation, and never-ending hope, followed inevitably by frustration and disappointment, with just enough triumph to keep the addiction fed.

The source of some of my mother's finest horticultural treasures was an eccentric and brilliant dealer named Henry Landis. Six months before my mother died, Landis died mysteriously in his home, apparently the victim of murder. Childless, he had named his sister as his heir. Her inheritance consisted of his ordinary North York bungalow, backed by a garden filled with the most exceptional and rare hybrid plants, worth a fortune far surpassing the value of the house. The sister wished to remove the treasures from the garden and sell them to dealers. But she knew nothing about plants, and feared that she would be taken advantage of. She appealed to my mother, whom she knew to be a client of her brother's, to help her estimate the value of what she had. As a thank-you gesture (my mother's educated eye had encouraged the sister to ask for and receive prices more than triple what she had first been offered) she invited my mother to select some of her favourites as a gift. Since it was too late in the fall to transplant them safely, they agreed that my mother would return in the spring to collect them. In the meantime, my mother tied pieces of white ribbon around the plants and shrubs of her choice, to show that they were spoken for.

When spring arrived, my mother was dead. Henry Landis's sister insisted on keeping her promise to my mother all the same, and invited my father to collect the plants my mother had wanted. My father, finding this task too painful, sent Tony and me instead. The white ribbons were blowing in a fresh spring breeze, the promise of new life ready to burst from refreshed branches; a tangible reminder that my mother's struggle against time had been lost, and that death had triumphed over hope.

Barbara Frum on the box at Stratford

Chapter 12

The Journal Decade

BARBARA FRUM:

Thanks for talking to us.

HOWARD COSELL:

Barbara, this has been the greatest thrill of my career.

BARBARA FRUM:

Do you expect me to believe that?

HOWARD COSELL:

No, Barbara, but it would be great if you did.

THE JOURNAL, *July 1983*

ON HER WAY into work at *The Journal* one morning in November 1990, my mother discovered that she was booked for the sort of interview she most hated to do. The premier of Quebec, Robert Bourassa, had been operated on for skin cancer two months earlier, and was perhaps much sicker than had previously been reported. There was speculation that he might have to step down, striking, it was assumed, a devastating blow to federalist forces already fragile. The idea of someone being too sick to perform a critical job — and the disaster that might follow — was a subject my mother found threatening and depressing.

Don MacPherson, a reporter from the *Montreal Gazette*, was

scheduled to talk to my mother about the implications of Bourassa's illness. Sally Reardon, a senior editor at *The Journal*, remembers, "Barbara called the desk to talk about how we should handle the interview. As far as I was concerned, Don is the kind of reporter you can ask three questions and get three perfect answers. I assumed an interview with him was as simple as climbing onto a bicycle. I said, 'Oh, Barbara, it's just three minutes. Just ask all the standard questions.' There was a pause. 'Well,' she said, 'do you want to tell me what those are?'"

If genius is the ability to make something very difficult look easy, then my mother had a genius for asking questions. Her questions may have seemed to flow from each other with inevitable momentum. But that is not how it works. She never performed a "standard" interview in her career. "Every interview for Barbara was a difficult interview," Sally Reardon says, perhaps explaining how my mother became this country's best-loved journalist. She felt the weight of what she did.

My mother was forty-four when she was offered the position of host of *The Journal*, seven years older than she ever expected to be. Once she accepted the job, she became, in the words of media analysts, "the most powerful woman in Canadian broadcasting." But despite the allure of such a position, my mother had been hesitant to accept the job. She worried about the effect the pressures and demands of the program would place on her health and life, and she was sceptical of the feasibility of a program as ambitious and untested as *The Journal*. On the second point she was not alone. Much of the Canadian public and many of Canada's television critics shared her reticence. A week before its debut, Jim Slotek wrote in the *Ottawa Citizen*: "*The Journal*...could turn out to be the biggest white elephant in the history of the CBC." In the *Toronto Star*, Jim Bawden quoted a caustic CBC insider, who said "it will be the greatest radio show ever seen on CBC TV."

"People thought that this would be the Edsel of the CBC," says Peter Herrndorf, who was vice president of the English network in 1979, when *The Journal* was being put together.

The program was a response to the same sort of crisis that had brought *As It Happens* into being except this time it was the television network in trouble.

"TV was fussy and old-fashioned," says Herrndorf. "The question came up about whether or not the CBC mattered," (a question that seems to arise at the CBC at regular, ten-year intervals). "There was no doubt that a malaise had set in and it was important to break out of it."

To do this, Herrndorf recruited three of the leading men in news and current affairs — Vince Carlin, English language news chief; Bill Morgan, head of current affairs; and Mark Starowicz, who at age thirty-five was still a whiz kid producer — to devise a rescue plan. Herrndorf locked the men up in the Four Seasons Hotel in Yorkville and gave them "subpoena powers to call on anyone at the CBC to put this thing together. . . . It seemed to them like they were locked up for three years but it was actually three or four weeks."

There emerged a radical and expensive plan. *The National* would be moved from its 11:00 p.m. slot where it had resided for almost thirty years. It would be married to a live, forty-minute, prime-time, current affairs program.

"We wanted to take the 10:00 to 11:00 p.m. period and make it 'must watching'. Go head-to-head with U.S. programming," says Herrndorf. "People thought this was a suicidal gamble." The new show would be competing with such American mega-hits as *Dynasty*, *Hill Street Blues*, *Lou Grant*, and *Hart to Hart*. "People thought we were unbelievably presumptuous, but the phrase we often used when thinking of the show we wanted to create was 'a sense of occasion'." Others used the phrase "leap of faith".

On behalf of *The Journal,* resources were bled away from some of the CBC's old stalwarts, while other programs were just killed off. Although Herrndorf says that *The Journal* was "poverty stricken by satellite standards," it nonetheless gobbled $9 million in start-up costs, and required an operating budget in the neighbourhood of $18 million a year.

Mark Starowicz, the newly appointed executive producer of *The Journal,* told a reporter that when the resource-devouring program began, "we were the most hated unit in the country."

Herrndorf says that after securing the money to create *The Journal,* "the next step was to recruit Barbara Frum. The debate wasn't about whether or not it should be Barbara Frum, only about who the team around her would be."

But, "when we came to Barbara at first," he explains, "she said she wouldn't host *The Journal* under any circumstances and sent us packing."

Mark Starowicz has a different memory of that process. "Richard Bronstein [the senior producer] and I wanted Barbara Frum. We fought for her. Not with Peter, who was high up and supportive, but there were opponents. There were forces who wanted Patrick Watson, and there were higher managers who doubted her television skills. Some very powerful figures in journalism were fighting very hard to get that job. It was a struggle. Doubly so when Barbara turned us down."

Even without her private reasons, it would be easy to understand my mother's hesitation. In the ten years that she had hosted *As It Happens,* she had acquired an enviable journalistic reputation, interviewed every world figure worth talking to, and had a huge amount of fun. "My sense of myself had fused with [*As It Happens*] to such a degree," she told Mike Boone of the *Montreal Gazette,* "that I wasn't sure if I existed outside the studio. It occurred to me that I had found such a perfect niche for myself that to even consider anything else was ludicrous."

On *As It Happens* my mother did ten stories a night. On *The Journal* she would get to do two if she was lucky. "I laugh so much in this job," she would say appreciatively of *As It Happens*. At *The Journal* she knew a more sober atmosphere would prevail. On *As It Happens* she could show up to work in an old sweater with a clashing shade of lipstick. At *The Journal* she would be sucked into a vortex of hair and teeth, makeup and clothes, all leeching attention from her intellectual and journalistic intentions. On *As It Happens* she was home by 9:00 p.m. at night. *The Journal* would keep her at work until 11:00 or later, with no significant increase in salary.

Persuading my mother to choose the wrong option for each of these cases was a job that fell to Starowicz.

"The dynamic was about comforting somebody who worried about being controlled and diminished by technology," Starowicz remembers. He brought my mother into the new *Journal* studio to show her around. "What I was trying to do was show her where she'd sit. It was the worst thing I could have done. She started acting really uncomfortable, really nervous. She wanted to get out. She was worried about being 'crushed by technology' — that was her phrase. And, like an idiot, all I did was show her nothing but the technology."

It was the technology, however, that made my mother the ideal candidate. As everyone in Canada eventually realized, she could not actually see many of the people she was interviewing on the screen. She had to pretend that she could see them — to do a radio interview with make-up. She was, after all, an experienced *radio* interviewer.

"It was to a great extent bogus," says Herrndorf of this technology. "We played with eye contact to make it look real. We were concerned with the ethics of it: we were pretending about a lot of things...but we felt it was legitimate because we were not distorting the content."

When Starowicz told the *Saskatoon Star-Phoenix*, "There are people who think that Barbara Frum will not translate well from radio to television," he might have been expressing my mother's anxieties. She feared failure as an actress. Her reputation was based on her naturalness, ease, the honesty of her emotions. Wouldn't these qualities be lost on television?

And yet, just because my mother's impulse was to say "no", it was inevitable that her psyche would demand she say "yes". She could never forgive herself for timidity. It was too late in her life to be held back by fear. After private deliberation, she decided to sign on to "the biggest gamble in Canadian broadcasting history."

With characteristic grace, my mother's first action after accepting the job was to climb into her car and drive with my father to Alan Maitland's farm, outside Toronto. Maitland had been her co-host on *As It Happens*; she did not want him to read about the end of their partnership in the newspapers. After six happy years sharing a tiny recording cubicle, she felt she owed this to "Lord Maitland of Snacks".

"Leaving *As It Happens*," she told the *Montreal Gazette* shortly after accepting the new position, "was like getting divorced from myself."

When Mary Lou Finlay was selected as co-host of *The Journal*, a dramatic barrier was crossed. It would be the first time in CBC history — perhaps in the history of any network in the world — that two women would front a network's flagship program. (And what a long way from the final episode of *The Way It Is*.) Finlay was recruited from CTV's *Live It Up*. She had previously hosted CBC's *Take 30*.

"When we picked Mary Lou as the co-host, advancing two women as anchors, believe me, *most* of the CBC thought we were nuts," Starowicz recalls. "A 'radio host' and on top of that, two women. It was unprecedented. It was a *beau risque*."

The shock of two women sharing an anchor desk became a talking point. Reviewing *The Journal*'s opening broadcast in the *Toronto Sun*, Bob Pennington wrote, "the major victory was for... feminists. I was delighted that two women should front a program that is not only crucial to the future of our national network but Canadian broadcasting in general."

Although they couldn't admit it out loud, many Canadians did not adapt so easily. *The Royal Canadian Air Farce* toyed with the nation's discomfort in a number of radio sketches in which Luba Goy impersonated both my mother and Mary Lou with exactly the same voice, hinting at catty discord.

My mother and Finlay had a great deal of respect for each other. I honestly never heard my mother say a word against her harsher than, "Mary Lou is wearing pink again today which means I'm stuck wearing blue!"

In turn, Finlay's affection for my mother was laid bare when, upon hearing the news of my mother's death on her car radio, she raced to my parents' house and embraced my father, brother and me. Then, looking around and noticing that she was almost alone with our grieving family — it was still very early in the morning — said, "I'm so sorry for barging in but I just didn't know what to do with myself!"

Although Finlay occupied the position of co-host for only two years before choosing to become a *Journal* field reporter, the cause was not any trouble in the studio, but rather Starowicz's growing realization that a forty-minute show was too short to justify two full-time hosts.

The Journal first went to air on January 11, 1982. Far short in quality from what the show would become, it received decent if mixed reviews.

"There are still wrinkles to work out," said Bruce Blackadar in the *Toronto Star*, "but for a new baby it sure has a lusty cry." Rick

Groen wrote in the *Globe and Mail*, "In what is so far a decidedly hit and miss operation ... Barbara Frum has proven herself a skilful on-air general. Composed yet incisive, aggressive yet polite, she handles the performers' reins with graceful aplomb." Whereas the *Toronto Sun* offered: "Well, so that's CBC's *The* (yawn) *Journal*, huh?"

With prescience Mark Starowicz told the *Saskatoon Star-Phoenix*: "It's the beginning of a program that will be on for a decade."

The reviews, no matter how flattering or hostile, were less important to CBC brass than the size of the audience. Herrndorf had convinced himself and others that if the show could achieve a slow build of viewers — to perhaps 900,000 by the end of the first year — it could be considered a success. Numbers any lower would be humiliating. More than a few reputations depended on the results. Since *The Journal*'s debut pre-dated electronically-gathered overnight ratings, there was an excruciating wait for results. Two weeks passed before good news arrived: 1.8 million Canadians watched *The Journal*'s first night, building to 2.1 million by the first Friday — a 31 percent share of all viewers.

"Those numbers bought the show six months," says Herrndorf, "because the program still wasn't very good. The audience gave them the time they needed. Mark's biggest fear was that there would be an international incident too soon." Fortunately for Starowicz, not to mention the world, the first major international crisis after the start of *The Journal* did not occur until April of 1982, when Britain went to war in the Falkland Islands. "By then *The Journal* was ready," says Herrndorf.

If it took four months for the documentary units and field producers to get up to speed, it also took my mother time to polish her own performance. She had to shed nervous tics: shredding Kleenex between her fingers, picking hangnails, folding and refolding her hands. The first month was the worst.

Some early interviews were rough. During *The Journal*'s first week, it was announced that the British Columbian serial killer, Clifford Olsen, had received $100,000 in exchange for showing police where he had buried the bodies of his victims. That night, my mother interviewed the mother of one of the victims. I am not trying to mock this woman, only to give a sense of how choppy those early shows could be.

BARBARA FRUM:

Some people are frightened to reward a murderer for such hideous crimes as the most terrible thing they've ever heard.

MOTHER:

Well, I don't know that much about the law.

BARBARA FRUM:

But as [a mother] it hasn't offended you?

MOTHER:

No.

BARBARA FRUM:

Are you . . .

MOTHER:

It's better . . . pardon?

BARBARA FRUM:

Sorry, go ahead.

MOTHER:

It's better knowing, you know, like — excuse me — the space of time, like, okay . . .

"My memory of Barbara for the first six months was sheer intensity," says Ruth Ellen Soles, *The Journal*'s publicist as well as my mother's friend and confidant. "I had a sense that on a number of occasions she sat and watched tapes and said, 'I'll do this differently and I'll do that differently.' She spent the first six months constantly trying to figure out how to do it better. She worked harder than anyone I have ever seen."

"She had crushing responsibilities, and she felt them deeply," my brother David says. "When she joined *The Journal* she became the paramount explainer to the country of itself." My mother thought *The Journal* not just a news outlet but also a forum for national unity and understanding, and a source of national identity.

"I believe the swift and generous acceptance of *The Journal* beginning from the very first week last January, vindicates Canadians," she said in an address at Dalhousie University in November 1982. "It proves that Canadians have long wanted a program that reveals this country as an interesting place to live, as interesting as they had believed all along, in their heart of hearts, it really was. They have wanted for a long time a prime-time nightly program that takes them seriously, and takes Canada seriously."

My mother deeply respected her audience. While so much television today is distinguished by its patronizing stupidity, my mother operated under the assumption that her audience was intelligent and informed.

She was notorious for dragging herself into the studio from her dressing room at the last possible minute, even if it meant burning up expensive satellite time. She hoarded every second to prepare, and much of that preparation took place over the telephone.

"People who hadn't heard from her in five years would get urgent calls asking, 'what do you think about Russia?'" says Starowicz. "And the urgency of the call would make it all the more flattering. Barbara never pretended to know anything that she didn't actually know. She was unafraid to admit she needed help, which is a risky thing."

David's insights into how hard my mother worked arose from his own experience as an unofficial research assistant. Between 1984 and 1987 he attended Harvard Law School. He had foolishly complained to our mother that he was bored much of the time, and would receive research-related telephone calls from her as often as three times a week.

"When she called to say, 'We're doing a piece on Nicaragua, what can you tell me about it?' the information she would want would start with the sixteenth century, not two weeks ago," says David (whose degrees from Yale were in history).

"She was interested in the deep origins of things. To that extent we thought very similarly. So if we were talking about Nicaragua, we would talk about how many of the Sandinista leadership were white, and how many of the Contra leaders were Indian, and what that meant.

"If she asked me a question and I said to her, 'I don't think I know the answer to that,' there would be a pause until I said, 'but I guess I can find out.' Then I would go to Widener Library and spend an afternoon reading up on a subject, which I don't regret because I know a lot about many subjects that I wouldn't have otherwise."

It was her studious, almost un-television approach to journalism, I believe, that won my mother the respect of her audience. "There are so many people on television who are so similar to each other," says Robert Fulford. "Barbara was irregular. She had an edginess to her. She was trying to get so much out of an interview that she was never totally self-controlled the way ninety-nine out of one hundred television people are. They have this one little question they are going to ask. They are not going to look foolish for one second. It may be the most banal, fatuous question on earth but they'll never look silly. Barbara looked silly sometimes."

Part of my mother's job, especially in the beginning, when people were still getting used to the technology, was to prevent her guests from feeling silly. This was sometimes difficult. To conduct a "double-ender", the subject must stare into the reflective glass of a camera, and talk animatedly and unselfconsciously to a mirror image of his own face. Some early guests were overwhelmed. One of them was, curiously enough, the actor, Donald Sutherland.

In February 1983, Sutherland was in town to promote his new film, *Threshold*, and it was arranged that he be interviewed from his suite at the Four Seasons Hotel. (The technology was still so fresh and thrilling, that even when guests were in Toronto, or in the *CBC itself, The Journal* still insisted on using its double-ender technology. It took time to admit that face-to-face interviews, when possible, were still preferable.) As the crew set up around him, Sutherland asked to be introduced to the interviewer. When the concept of a double-ender was explained to him, Sutherland was so uncomfortable that he refused to continue. My mother was summoned to the telephone to charm and cajole him. She got him to agree, but he insisted that at the very minimum, he needed to know what my mother was wearing. In her attempt to jolly him up, she is said to have responded, "Mr. Sutherland, I am wearing absolutely nothing. Didn't they tell you about the format of this program?" An unremarkable interview followed.

Although she often complained about never getting to do "fun" interviews after she left *As It Happens*, my mother also told me, "I hate interviewing movie stars. All you ever get out of them is extruded plastic. I've never had a successful interview with a movie star."

This and other observations about her career were made during an interview I conducted for a 1990 book called *The Newsmakers*. The book began as "a favour" to my mother. A *Journal* cameraman, Jean Guy Nault, had been severely injured on the job and was paralyzed for life. My mother and many of her *Journal* colleagues, particularly Ann Medina and Bill Cameron (who had worked most closely with Nault), were looking for a suitable project to raise money for him. My mother suggested that I put

together a popular anecdotal book about Canadian news corre-
spondents, with all royalties assigned to Nault and family.

In retrospect, my own valuable payment was a precious audio-
tape — the interview with my mother for the book.

Without realizing it — this was certainly not the conscious
design of my interrogation of her — all of the anecdotes my mother
gave me for *The Newsmakers* revolved around one theme: the ways
in which prominent people handle their power.

For example, the former secretary of state under Reagan,
George Shultz, stood out in her memory as one of the most "decent
and ordinary" men she had encountered. An obscure choice, but
there it is.

> When television moves in they can really make a mess. We
> interviewed Shultz in his suite of offices in the State Depart-
> ment, and by the time he arrived for his interview, he was
> flabbergasted by the muck we'd made of his place. I said, "How
> do you like the remodeling we've done here, Mr. Shultz?" and
> he grimaced. But then he went around and shook hands with
> every member of the crew; and, at the end, he did the same
> thing. Most people will shake hands with the interviewer and
> maybe the director. But this man shook hands with every
> lighting-man, the grip, the cameramen. I'd never seen such
> civility before.

An interview with Jimmy Carter in October 1982, a year after
he failed to win a second term in the White House, was memorable
for what could be gleaned of the psychological struggle to adjust to
the loss of so much power.

> With Jimmy Carter, we could have stayed a week. He had
> rented himself the top floor of the local federal building in

Atlanta. When you entered, you saw the roster of tenants.
There was one plaque which read "President Jimmy Carter". I
appreciate that in the United States you never lose a title once
you've had it, but there was something so poignant about seeing his name on the roster like that. You get off the elevator
and there's this enormous plaque that reads President Jimmy
Carter. You get to his door and it says Office of President
Jimmy Carter. Wherever there was a blank space there was a
brass plaque that reminded you that you were at the office of
President Jimmy Carter.

The American ambassador to the United Nations, Jeanne Kirkpatrick, kept *The Journal* "waiting like nobody had ever kept us
waiting" and thereby provoked deep hostility.

"I have found that when someone important keeps you waiting they tell you why and give you some idea of how long it will be,"
she told me. "That's fine. But we were told, 'We don't know when
she's coming, or where she is.'"

She believed that Kirkpatrick's rude and inconsiderate behaviour — my mother and the crew had flown to New York for the
interview and were expected back in Toronto for that evening's
show — was because "she is a classic over-compensating female."
She was behaving, my mother believed, with more aggression and
hostility than a man in her position would dare exhibit.

Kirkpatrick is certain that the whole world despises her and
she must have especially hated the idea that a woman who
would know her route — because chances are the woman interviewing her had also had to fight the same route — would be
even less sympathetic to her. She had such a snappish reputation it was as though you were to interview the mock turtle in
Alice in Wonderland. Her aide was so frightened of her that

when Kirkpatrick came down half an hour later, [he barked at us] "Get in your chairs! Get set up! Here she comes!" She came in and sat down and turned her face to me and said: "That's a pretty blouse. And that's a pretty pin." Girl talk from the mock turtle. And, I thought, is that supposed to be disarming? I thought the logical first sentence would have been I am so sorry to have kept you waiting for two-and-a-half hours.

Politicians had nothing on entertainers. In 1989, my mother and a crew from *The Journal* flew to New York to interview Paul McCartney at the Plaza Hotel. He was on a press junket to promote his film, *Goodbye to Broadstreet*, and my mother's interview was scheduled for five o'clock.

He did some interviews in the morning and then went to the Plaza Room with his wife Linda for lunch. They decided to have a long lunch. They couldn't care less that they had twenty-five journalists waiting for them upstairs. We had to wait about four extra hours. I guess it must have amused them to be so indifferent. It seems to me that when you are hustling a movie you do what's required. But not Paul McCartney. I found it very awkward because his little gig was that before you sat down to interview him, you got your picture taken with Paul McCartney. So he put his arm around you and his cameraman took your picture and he mailed you an autographed "pic". Everyone on *The Journal* crew wanted a picture of him. So there's another long pause while a million Polaroids and automatic flashbulbs go off. Then autographs. My face must have been as green as pea soup by the time we sat down. This performance was much better than the interview. I was struck by his presumption that any female of a certain age would be water on the pavement before him. I think that I was so embarrassed to be cast as a groupie that it wasn't a very good interview. I thought he was extremely pretty, but very arrogant and in love with himself.

She was touched by the modesty of Paul Simon, however, even though niceness in a celebrity doesn't guarantee a nice interview.

I just loved the Graceland album and worked very hard on my interview with Paul Simon. He's terminally shy. My producer was really in love with him, and she was very disheartened when she saw he had a hairpiece. I didn't notice it, but I wasn't looking at him the way she was.

Before and after the interview, he was wonderful. He told us a charming story about performing at the Apollo Theater in Harlem on tour for Graceland. He was being honoured by the theatre and it was a great moment for him. But, as he told us, when it came time for him to get on stage, the master of cere-monies launched into an enormous, womped-up introduction, which ended with: "Here he is. The man you've all been wait-ing for. The great, the incomparable — Neil Simon!"

We were charmed by this story but, when we went to do the interview, he was like a monk who has taken a vow of silence. He wouldn't say a word. Finally, I just said to him: "Don't you know how much we all love this album?" But he couldn't put the praise anywhere. It couldn't nourish him. He was full of angst. I liked him and I liked the album, but he was quite mis-erable, and he was taking his misery out on me.

He answered in yeses and nos. I ran out of questions quickly and quit. There's just a limit to the number of one-word answers you can run in a row. Two or three, okay, but then you need a longer one.

Failures like that used to kill me, now they make me laugh. After a while you just say to yourself, how bad can it get? You go for your personal worst. A bad interview isn't amusing, but a grotesquely appalling one is. You pass a line when enough good has gone by, you can tolerate a little bad.

Though she claimed not to have had any success interviewing movie stars, Peter Gzowski was once moved to write my mother a "fan letter" after he heard an interview she did with Shirley MacLaine in 1985. Gzowski himself had interviewed MacLaine earlier that day on *Morningside*, an experience he had found totally unsatisfactory. When my mother received his letter, Gzowski explained, "she trotted by with her little dog and held out the letter and asked, 'What does this mean?'"

Gzowski had to tell her defensively, "Barbara, I thought you did a great piece!" He couldn't explain her reaction. "My letter was written with total adulation."

"She was suspicious?" I asked Gzowski.

"I think so, yes. But I don't know what she could be suspicious of."

My mother, a born sceptic, analyzed people's actions and comments with perhaps excessive scrutiny. Praise made her especially wary. But when I found Gzowski's letter saved in her files, I knew that she would have been touched:

Barbara:

"I honestly don't know how to deal with you..." (or some facsimile thereof) is one of the greatest opening questions, in my humble view...just the perfect what-I'd-say-if-I'd-been-there that we all try for. Unfortunately for me, I had been there yesterday morning, and never quite found the handle you found. (She's an unfunny dip-stick, isn't she, for a dip-stick?)

Anyway, I thought I'd tell you that. I seldom stay up late enough to watch you in action, but when I do it sure is good to see what great form you're in and how, even though radio is better than television, you're still the queen.

Your fan, Gzowski

Because my mother's greatest respect was reserved for those in power who retained modesty and integrity, one of the most important encounters of her career, and life, was with Nelson Mandela. She interviewed him in South Africa, after he was released from prison in February 1990.

She was not expecting to be touched. "Barbara did not want to go to South Africa," Mark Starowicz remembers. "She was not about to swallow anything that came out of Mandela's mouth. She was very concerned about the township violence. She had gone to a couple of meetings about South Africa organized by a group here and she thought there was a lot of naivety going on about South Africa. And then, there she is in front of Mandela's home, more moved than anybody on the spot. She couldn't stop talking about South Africa after that. As she said on air during her stand-up: 'I feel privileged to be here.'"

From the moment she met Mandela she was conscious of his nobility — his authenticity, decency, moral fortitude, incorruptibility.

On the tenth anniversary show of *The Journal* she explained, in part, why she had been so moved.

A gorgeous new white house had been built for Nelson Mandela's return by Winnie Mandela and yet he insisted on meeting the journalists of the world in the backyard of his humble bungalow from where it all started...What the whole world wanted to know, of course, in those first hours after Nelson Mandela was released, was would this man be broken by prison and, of course, for many of the years of the twenty-seven he was in, he was under extraordinary conditions. But this man emerged with enormous discipline, but above all, with enormous dignity, and he touched everyone who met him that first day.

After recording 2,600 editions of *The Journal,* I think it is fair to say that the interviews my mother best appreciated on television were, in the end, the same type she had appreciated on radio: those with people who had been through a terrible ordeal and had come out nobly. David Jacobson was an example: the American held in a Beirut cellar for five years; or Susan Nelles, the nurse falsely accused of murder, whose strength of character my mother admired; or the selfless survivors of a military transport plane that crashed in the Arctic, saving each other's lives at great risk; or the young female lawyer who waged a successful but emotionally harrowing legal battle on behalf of "Nancy B", a severely handicapped woman from Quebec who wished to end her own life by being removed from her respirator.

"The greatest compliment that an interviewer can be paid," says Gzowski, "is when listeners say: 'You asked exactly what was on my mind.' The danger is that when you yourself become a star and have your privacy invaded, your allegiance can switch until you're too sympathetic, especially of political figures. I find that. I always back off questions that I wouldn't want asked of me. I don't know how Barbara dealt with that."

As the Don MacPherson interview showed, my mother didn't flinch from a question when it needed to be asked (she did not fail to ask MacPherson what effect the rumours of Bourassa's ill heath had on Quebec politics). But it is my view that she dealt with the potentially corrupting influence of her own celebrity in two ways.

The first was by keeping a studious distance from politicians. "When Mulroney was elected," Starowicz recalls, "Barbara was invited to his house, as was every other journalist, but she declined the invitation. I remember her holding it in front of me and saying, 'I'm not going to go!'" My mother felt it was a breech of journalistic ethics to socialize with politicians and strictly avoided temptations.

The second way was by refusing to imagine herself as a star. Many readers may think this a naive and fawning remark. But my mother's attitude to fame was unusual. There probably had been a time when she wished to be a star. Her good friend Robert Fulford believes this to be obvious. "I always say that only those who want to become well-known become well-known, except for criminals and billionaires. The rest want to and like it."

Near the beginning of her career when she started on television, she may have enjoyed that heady leap into recognition. I remember once when I was young, being with her when she bumped into someone on the street with whom she was brusque. Afterward, I said to her, "You were very rude to that woman, you know." My mother replied, "What you have to understand Linda, is that there are a lot of people out there who never gave me the time of day when they thought I was just a stupid, boring housewife. Now when they want to be my friend I refuse to be nice." That is a side of fame that anyone can appreciate: the prestige and the opportunity to settle old grievances.

However, I don't believe that she cared enough about such payoffs to make the pursuit of fame a goal in itself. Early in her days on *As It Happens*, she wrote to David, "The approval and admiration of others are traps. They can sicken your soul. Make you dependent. They can cripple your chance for independence, force you to make wrong choices because you need the fix of other people's respect and secret envy."

Fame, if you had a sense of responsibility, and my mother did, was a burden. When she was at *The Journal*, she received dozens of letters daily; not just fan mail, but letters of complaint, of correction, of request, and of attack. For the first few years, she sent sometimes lengthy, always hand-written replies to all. Eventually, she was persuaded to hire a secretary to type dictated responses.

"Barbara was particularly vulnerable to letters from ordinary people, which sounds like a sentimental statement but that was the long and the short of it," Starowicz remembers. "Precious few standard letters went out."

Viewers who wrote to say that they were worried because she was looking tired or pale, would often receive a direct and reassuring telephone call, particularly if they were elderly and female, and my mother knew they would fret.

"One of the hardest and most time-consuming elements of my job," remembers Ruth Ellen Soles, "was the number of people I had to turn down on her behalf. We both agreed that the *way* she turned people down was more important than saying yes. This is a small thing but it says a lot about her. Everybody's request, she understood, was as important as the sun and the moon. When she had to say 'no' to something, there had to be a long explanation as to why. It was really important that the person understood that the request had been considered and, if at all possible, fulfilled, or if not, a reason why it could not be.

"In fact, the last few years when everybody except Barbara decided that it was okay if she said 'no' by just saying 'no', I would have to coach her to say: 'I can't and I won't.' And she would say, 'Yeah, I'll say that and then I'll explain . . .' And I'd say, 'No, no, no. In this case you'll simply say: I can't.' And we'd have to rehearse this. And she'd have to practise saying it back to me six times."

"There was much more of a connection between her private life and her public life," says Gzowski. "I have a much wider gap between the public persona and the private persona. I'm known for being sarcastic and tough. But she wasn't. She was genuinely nice. My kids have a running joke that they're going to tape-record me and expose me for the charlatan that I am."

Even Starowicz, who is known for a temperamental, curmudgeonly approach to office politics, admired this quality of my mother's. "Often I'd get angry about an interview, or something, that was a function of a bad briefing, or the feeding of an incorrect fact, and I'd go through the roof. And then there would be a call from Barbara telling me that this person's mother was sick, or they had a strain in their marriage. And I would say, 'Well I have strains too; that doesn't mean I get facts wrong.' And she would say, 'Why don't you just cool it, Mark?' And yet she was the one who was made to look like a fool in the studio. Not me, or the producer who had made the mistake."

"She knew everybody who had the slightest problem in the unit," Starowicz continues. "She would find out who was pregnant first, who had Hodgkin's disease first, she was the first to know who was gay."

My mother radiated an empathic understanding that made people want to confide in her. One producer tells the story of being in my mother's dressing room to brief her on an upcoming interview. The producer was distraught but doing her best to hide it. Apparently she did not do it well enough to prevent my mother from looking at her and saying gently: "So, how are things going with your stepchildren?" There was an outpouring of tears and heartache.

"She really tried to understand every person she came into contact with," says producer Sally Reardon, whose first insight into my mother's gentle character happened after the taping of an interview during the Lebanon war in October 1984, when two hundred American Marines died in a suicide bombing attack on their barracks. Since the interview had to be done extremely early in the morning, it was recorded over the telephone at my mother's home. After it was over, the cameraman picking up the images in Beirut told Reardon that he did not intend to send the tape to Damascus for an arranged satellite-feed. For his own reasons, he would send it to Tel Aviv where new arrangements would have to be made.

As Reardon remembers it: "The day suddenly became a lot harder and it wasn't even nine o'clock. 'Never mind,' Barbara says, 'let's go outside and sit for a minute.' I follow Barbara through the house. She's trying to distract me from the worries of the interview. If Barbara can attempt to be so gracious, I can at least make an attempt, too. I look at the wall and recognize a Jack Bush painting. I make my stab at graciousness: 'Gosh, Barbara,' I gush, 'that's a lovely Bush.' Barbara, who is leading the way through a set of doors onto a patio, looks down at what can only be described charitably as a twig stuck in a pot of dirt. A lone leaf is the only sign that somewhere inside that pathetic thing life still has some kind of hold. And then, with a gesture as tender as any I will ever see, Barbara holds the leaf between two fingers. She says: 'Yes, it's coming along very nicely, isn't it?' It was at that moment that I lost my heart to Barbara Frum."

My mother was not only kind to the people with whom she had daily contact, but to all who fell within her orbit. When a technician told my mother that one of the documentary editors — someone my mother had never worked with — had a wife who was dying of cancer, my mother called the editor to ask if she could help. She wanted to know which doctors his wife was seeing, what medications she was on, and what the editor and his wife were doing to sustain themselves emotionally. "What you really need to do," my mother told him when she learned his wife had not much longer to live, "is to spend time together." Shortly after, she arranged to have an honorarium from a speaking engagement handed over so that the editor and his wife could take a last trip to Jamaica.

The net was cast wider. Another example happened in Russia, where *The Journal* went for a week in November 1989, to do what many of my mother's colleagues believe was the best work of her career. It was an exciting moment in Russian history. The walls of repression were only beginning to tumble and it was unclear whether the liberalization would be permanent or just a brief reprieve. It was still dangerous for those interviewed to practise their newly acquired free speech. One of the most candid, therefore brave, interview subjects was a young translator named Dasha, perhaps thirty, a single mother with a six-year-old son. My mother interviewed Dasha in the tiny apartment where she lived with son and parents. My mother was touched by her dignity, intelligence, and grace despite cramped living quarters, a miserable income, shortages of food, medicine, and everything else.

BARBARA FRUM:

When will it be good to be young here?

DASHA RISHKOV:

When? I think that when young people change themselves. I don't know. Perhaps my son's generation will be different. Perhaps they will believe in anything. Because, you know, it is difficult because we are slaves. We are just slaves. And they, perhaps they will not be slaves. We are slaves and we are children of slaves. And there is a slavery in our heart and our soul. So perhaps they will not be slaves.

BARBARA FRUM:

If you could be like a magician, walk out tomorrow morning and the world was the way you wanted it, what would it look like?

DASHA RISHKOV:

I want to see friendly faces. I want to see people smiling to each other. I want to see people who believe in each other. And I want to — to see people who want to help and whom I want to help. And I want children to be taught some eternal things in their childhood, like what is kindness and what is good and what is . . . well, everything, you know?

Upon her return from Moscow, my mother went to a drugstore to pick up thank-you gifts for Dasha and three of her friends whom my mother had also interviewed. She bought enough aspirin, children's cough medicine, vitamins, and most valuable of all, condoms (equivalent to gold in the Russian private market) to fill a duffel bag.

"You can imagine what the cashier was thinking," my mother said to me as she packed the bag. "I've been shopping there for twenty-five years and all of a sudden I want to buy four hundred condoms."

After my mother's death, I found a series of letters from Dasha, thanking my mother for continued kindnesses. One read:

Dear Barbara!

I am writing to you to say I am so grateful. Thank you for wonderful letter regarding your broadcast from the S.U. Thanks a lot for all medicine you've sent us — it was so kind of you. Peter enjoyed all his children's vitamins — they taste like sweets . . . " Another letter: "You were so kind to send me the article by Brodsky. It was so pleasant for me that you didn't forget our talk about this essay and found time to do it. . . . I thought a lot about your offer to help me. I realized that it can be not very easy and besides I don't know all your possibilities. But the most important thing for me is to find out if there is a chance of getting me a job in North America. . . .

"There are some people who work very hard at becoming famous," Ruth Ellen Soles told me. "She worked very hard at becoming Barbara. I don't believe she wanted to be famous. But did she want to be remembered? You bet. Since her death I have come to realize why she did so many of the things she did: I think she really, really wanted to be remembered and I think she was very concerned about *how* she would be remembered. She didn't want to be a star, she wanted to be the very best journalist, and the very best person."

And yet for all her many kindnesses, it remained a running joke between my mother and me how diffident she could be to people who fawned over her. They would ask, "So, how do you handle the long hours?" and she would nod at them as though she were hearing-impaired, and say, smiling, "Thanks," and slink away. Then she would turn to me and say: "I know, I know. You're ashamed of your mother. I was really rude just then, wasn't I?" And I would respond, "Actually, no, that time wasn't too bad."

"When Barbara was approached by people saying fawning things to her, she was a bit of a fumble-bum," Starowicz agrees. "She actually did not know what to do."

I never saw her revel in her fame. Once, during one of many lunches on Church Street around the corner from *The Journal* offices, a waiter hovered, constantly refilling our glasses with water, checking how we were enjoying our food, smoothing our tablecloth.

"It certainly pays to have lunch with my beautiful daughter," she said with the pride of a Jewish Mamma. "Look at all the attention we're getting."

"Mum," I laughed. "It's not for me, it's for you!"

"Nonsense!" she said in wilful disbelief. "The waiter can't take his eyes off you."

"Don't you know you're a famous TV star?" I asked her. Of course she did know. But she never knew it too much.

"She used to be astonished," agrees Ruth Ellen, "that she was as recognizable as she was and that people held her in such high regard and looked to her for the things that they did. Sometimes I wanted to say, 'come off it, *you* know!' But she did seem genuinely surprised."

One thing that helped to keep her modest, was that she never became too powerful. There was the time, as Deirdre Kelly reported in a gossip column in the *Globe and Mail*, that my mother, hurrying out of a speaking engagement at Trinity College in downtown Toronto, was so late and frantic to get back to the studio, she actually jumped into someone's car on St. George Street and demanded to be taken to the CBC. According to Kelly, the driver of the car refused.

Days later, the co-ordinator of the event at Trinity wrote an indignant letter denying Kelly's story, suggesting that it was nasty and inaccurate.

"That was nice of that girl to write that letter, huh, Mum? I knew that story just didn't sound like you."

"Yes it was," said my mother, lifting an eyebrow. "But actually..."

"Actually?"

"Actually...Deirdre had it right."

"Pardon me?"

"I did exactly what she said I did."

"You did?"

A sheepish look came over her: "I did." We both erupted in shocked laughter.

"You actually jumped into someone's car and said: 'Take me to the CBC!'"

My mother's face lit up with embarrassment.

"I'm afraid so. I don't know what came over me."

The January before my mother died, *The Journal* celebrated its tenth anniversary. It was a bittersweet time for my mother. That she had lived to accomplish so much was a source of great joy. But the status of *The Journal* had suddenly become precarious. The office was awash in rumours — accurate ones — that the news department was plotting to annex *The Journal* to make a unified news hour (as they eventually did with *Prime Time News*). It was hard for my mother not to take this threat personally. Her strength was visibly ebbing away. She had been forced to take extended breaks from work because of a persistent flu. She began to fear that her wan appearance, unreliable voice, and even less reliable attendance would be good excuses to cancel her contract when it came up for renewal in June. She feared the truth of what critics were saying — that she was looking too tired. The idea terrified her. "They're going to fire me, Linda," she would say despondently. "They're getting ready to fire me." At first I would argue with her because I had a hard time believing there could be any truth to her fears. But my mother would become impatient. She didn't say things she didn't mean and she expected to be taken seriously.

In subsequent conversations, I tried to convince my mother that, if she did get fired, she had to remember that a television career wasn't everything. There were all kinds of worthwhile things she could do. She might, I suggested, return to her true love, radio, where it didn't matter what you looked like, or how much hair you did or didn't have because of chemotherapy. (My mother never did have chemotherapy but she was anticipating it.) Or she could write a book.

I remember vividly one weekend in February, a month before she died (I'm amazed to think I was sitting there with her, not understanding how little time was left), sharing some ideas I had for a television documentary I hoped to produce. It was then that my mother said to me perhaps the saddest thing I had ever heard from her: "Maybe I can work with you on that?"

It's not quite what she said — although it is that — but *how* she said it, like a little girl asking an older sister if she could join in a game of hopscotch.

Work and survival were connected in her mind: she honestly felt that without work she would die. And so, she would force herself to go to work when she was terribly ill.

At her memorial service, Mark Starowicz paid tribute to her tenacity, although I'm not sure he understood how much of that tenacity came from a desire to prove to him that she was still capable of doing her job:

On the eve of the Gulf War, Barbara got laryngitis. She was energetic and eager to work but she sounded hopelessly hoarse. At two in the morning, after our Pacific edition and a grueling night, I had to go up and tell her that we'd have to take her off the air until her voice cleared up.

"Barbara," I said. "You know in baseball the manager walks out to the mound when the pitcher's arm is getting tired?"

"No," she said, looking at me blankly. Barbara was not a big baseball fan.

She said: "You can't take me off the air — there's going to be a war."

I said: "The switchboards have been lit up with people saying to let you go home and rest. Go home, Barbara."

Then, within forty-eight hours, the wall of TV monitors at *The Journal* came alive with the purple skies over Baghdad. The Gulf War was on. But that first night, as everyone raced about their tasks in *The Journal* office, as we desperately tried to reach our documentary unit, which was in the middle of the bombing of Baghdad, as we were linking Amman, Cairo, Jerusalem, and Washington — there was a woman rushing around, delivering wirecopy, answering the phone, logging feeds, and bringing coffee to the Main Desk.

If she couldn't be the host, then she'd be the copy clerk. Throughout the war she became Barbara Frum, researcher; Barbara Frum, production assistant; Barbara Frum, story editor. And if you were on the phone for hours to Brian Stewart in Dhahran, just trying to keep the line open and yourself awake, she'd push a plate of chicken nuggets under your face and whisper: "Ketchup?"

In the final phase of the war, she resumed her place in the chair.

In his speech accepting my mother's honorary doctorate at the University of Toronto, three months after her death, my father said, "Barbara once told an interviewer, who asked her whether her position on television made her powerful, that she felt like a drip of water landing on a rock — and that it was a very small drip and a very big rock. That drop of water has now run dry. But as long as it lasted, it was so fresh, so clear, so pure that it inspired a whole nation."

In Normandy, 1972

Chapter 13

Mother and Me

He knew the human heart — because his own heart
had been broken and remade by life events that sensi-
tized him, but left him vulnerable.

BARBARA FRUM, *October 1989*
Tribute to John Hirsch

TWO YEARS AFTER my graduation from McGill, in 1986, my
best friend's mother died. My friend was already twenty-nine years
old, the age I would eventually be when my own mother died. My
friend's attachment to her mother was fierce — it was one of many
things we had in common — and in the immediacy of her grief she
sobbed, "Had I known she was dying, I would not have wasted so
much time. I would have sat at her feet and listened."

These words had a profound effect on me. I *did* know that my
mother was dying, and had known for a long time. The terrible
knowledge was ever in the forefront of my mind. But it wasn't until
my friend spoke, that I knew what I must do with my anxiety. In
the time left to us, I would have as much of my mother as I could.

And so, when friends spent their Saturday nights dating and
party hopping, I spent mine with my parents at their home. In the

living room, my father would listen to opera at a deafening volume while catching up on the week's newspapers, and my mother and I would have long conversations in the dining room. My mother would sit with Diva in her lap, dragging her fingers through the dog's fur. "The best therapy!" she would declare. Although my mother hated to be kissed by her friends, or have any physical contact with strangers, with her family and her dog there was always touch. During our regular Sunday afternoon walks through the ravine behind her home, she would throw an arm around me, toss a misplaced lock of my hair into place, or press her shoulder against mine.

On our walks, no topic was ever off limits; nothing was too personal or private or taboo. She would tell me about her colleagues, and funny stories about the people she had interviewed that week. We would discuss and debate the books we were reading, movies we had seen, our friends, men, sex. She fascinated me with her anecdotes and she listened to mine with an attentiveness and enjoyment that drew me out of hiding. I sought her advice and counsel with a sense of privilege. As she once said of her friend, the theatre director John Hirsch: "He could find that string at the top of your head to pull you into a taller, better, nobler shape."

Our life experience was very different: she had married and gained all her sexual experience from the first and only man she had fallen in love with; and she had flown a single trajectory to professional satisfaction. I was still searching for the right man and the right career. And yet, her insights into love and marriage, careers and creativity were thoughtful and always relevant to me. She reassured me about my talents and bullied me into pushing myself harder. Once when I complained about the difficulties I was having putting together a radio documentary for CBC's *Ideas*, she said, "Of course it's hard. The only things worth doing in life are hard."

Although she wished me the security and peace she had found

in her marriage, she was never too dogmatic to imagine and sympathize with the choices I might make.

I earned her disapproval only rarely, as I did, in 1985, when I had occasion to interview Leonard Cohen. The day after I called my mother to report: the interview was not memorable, but afterwards Cohen, at work on his album *The Future*, and suffering from writers' block, had invited me to dinner. We then drove around Mount Royal in his rented Buick and he recited poetry. I giddily recounted the details to my mother.

Unimpressed, she interrupted drily: "Just tell me you *didn't*."

"I didn't."

"You *sure* you didn't?"

"I swear I didn't!"

"Well, don't. We're talking thousands of women here. Do you understand what I am telling you? *Thou*-sands! "

Still, it was her nature to question everything. It was my mother who said to me spontaneously on one of our walks when I was still in my twenties: "If you're not married by the time you're thirty-two, I think you should have a baby on your own. I really don't see what would be wrong with it, and besides, *I* can't wait much longer." (These conversations, though she would never know it, were part of the inspiration for a television documentary I co-produced after my mother's death, called *Ms Conceptions*, about women who choose to become single mothers.)

During the week, my mother and I would often grab lunch together. (I then lived only blocks away from her Yorkville hairdresser.) One of her favourite spots was Yorkville's Coffee Mill, not because of the quality of the food (although the goulash is delicious) but because of the sentimental place this café held in her affections. As she would recount with reverent praise, the Coffee Mill was the only place in Toronto which served espresso and cappuccino in the early sixties.

Wherever we were, I knew that the cue to my mother to start a story was to place a freshly poured, steaming cup of coffee in front of her.

Here's a typical one: A friend of my mother's, a woman in her early forties, had died of cancer. Six months later, the dead woman's lover invited two of the woman's closest friends to lunch. When they arrived at the restaurant, they found the lover seated at a table for four.

"Is someone else joining us?" they asked.

"Yes," he said. Then he pulled out a picture of the dead woman and placed it at the fourth setting. My mother paused here for effect; then asked, "Can you imagine?"

"I think it's very sweet."

"Are you crazy? It's absolutely cuckoo. What do you suppose the waiter was thinking?"

"I don't know," I said, identifying with the lover just as I knew she was identifying with the woman in the photo. "That man must have really loved that woman to do something so eccentric."

"Linda," said my mother with a tone and look to announce that an important life lesson was about to be imparted. "That kind of behaviour is nuts. That's all it is. You do not need to bring someone's picture to a restaurant to remember them!"

All mothers, either by commission or omission, are the sources of our fundamental truths. In her moving book, *Motherless Daughters*, Hope Edelman explains that a girl who loses her mother at a young age loses the role model she needs to teach her how to become a woman. She loses what Edelman calls the "motherline" of knowledge, which includes everything from childbirth to the proper composition of thank-you notes.

I may have received more "motherline wisdom" than I would have had I not been so acutely aware of fleeting time. Even in the hospital a few days before she died, my mother still had the energy to observe, "You look pretty but your lipstick isn't on straight. You must take care to cover your whole mouth evenly."

There was no point in arguing that I was too distraught to care. I knew when she said, "Take care to cover your mouth evenly," she was also saying, "Do not forget what I have taught you."

My mother taught me about friendship, not only through our own, but by the friendships she maintained through adult life. Alan Borovoy called her "the best *foul*-weather friend you could ever hope to have." While she counted on healthy friends to distract and amuse her, she went out of her way to be emotionally available to friends who carried the burdens she did.

An example was her conduct during her friend Judy LaMarsh's last months of life. LaMarsh was a member of her Corwin Avenue family (the LaMarsh house was less than a block away from the Rosbergs'); her careers in journalism and politics brought her regularly into my mother's world. When she learned that LaMarsh was dying of cancer — alone and broke — my mother mobilized her forces. Together with political organizer Nancy Jamieson, my mother made dozens of calls, appealing to LaMarsh's friends and associates to help pay for LaMarsh's rent, housekeeper, nurse and medication. My mother collected the money, contributed an equal amount of her own, and ensured that the last months were filled with material comfort and love. When LaMarsh died, my mother arranged to have the surplus funds donated to the University of Toronto Law School, where a scholarship was established in LaMarsh's name.

Although she patiently tended the dying, my mother had no time for people with petty ailments who didn't know enough to stay out of her way. "I always tell the people at *The Journal*, don't come near me if you're sick, and they always say, so selfishly, 'I'm not! I'm not!' and then they hack and cough and blow and spray germs all over me!" When I was sick with a cold or flu, my mother never offered sympathy, only warnings to keep clear. "You feel terrible? Stuffed up? Well I certainly hope you're not planning on visiting me!"

It was a different story however, when I was sick in a different way. When I was twenty-seven, my doctor found a lump in my breast — probably, she thought, benign, but maybe not. It had to come out. I was terrified of both cancer and surgery. This was exactly the kind of crisis my mother knew how to nurse me through.

On the day I was scheduled to receive a mammogram, I called her from the hospital waiting room. I hoped she would have something to say to cheer me up. Instead I received an unusually harried response: "This isn't a good time for me to talk, Linda. I'm going to have to go." I sat back in my chair wondering why, suddenly, she seemed so indifferent when I knew she was actually very concerned. Minutes later she breezed into the waiting room. When I expressed surprise, she smiled and said: "Where else did you think I had to go?" I hugged her and she held my hand. Minutes later, my father breezed in. And when my mother and I both expressed surprise, he said in what was becoming something of a skit, "Well, where else did you think I'd be?"

On the day of the surgery, my mother, too ridden with flu to join me at the hospital, insisted I call her from the waiting-room phone so that she could talk me through the moments of presurgical terror. My surgeon, I was informed, was an hour behind schedule because he had to do some unexpected "extra" surgery on his last patient (horror!), so my mother launched a wonderful diversionary tactic. She grabbed the book she happened to be reading at the moment, a biography of Napoleon III written by her friend John Bierman, and started to read it over the telephone. She skipped directly to the parts she knew would interest me: Napoleon's colourful romantic escapades and the tale of his loveless marriage to Eugénie.

After surgery (the lump was indeed benign) my father picked me up and drove me to my parents' house where I climbed into bed with my mother and her flu. As tears streamed down my face, and a sense of self-pity overwhelmed me, my mother continued to read aloud from where she had left off. When she sensed my attention drifting she said:

"Now, Linda, when Rosalina walks in here, don't tell her about what just happened to you, it will only make her jealous." I laughed at this allusion to our housekeeper's hypochondria. We loved Rosalina but were entertained by her complicated psychology. The good news was that jokes seemed funny again.

Then my mother called Rosalina into the bedroom, and told her, "Linda must have the flu too, she's not feeling well. Do you mind getting her a bowl of that delicious chicken soup you've been feeding me?"

Rosalina surveyed me suspiciously and began to explain that although we two *thought* we were sick, she was *really* very ill. She suspected a stomach tumour, arthritis, vertigo, and maybe a brain tumour too. My mother snapped her out of her reverie with a gentle request for some water, as it was time for her to take her medication.

"You and your pills, Mrs. Frum," Rosalina huffed.

After she left the room, my mother and I looked at each other. There we were: she dying of cancer, and me with a bleeding incision on a sensitive part of my body.

"You know that woman is going to live to a hundred and twenty don't you?" my mother said calmly.

"Yes, Mummy," I smiled. "I know." She picked up her book and continued to read to me.

Spending so much time with my mother did not leave my own life vacant. In 1986, I wrote a guidebook to Canadian universities which was condemned and praised in equal measure and brought me notoriety. It also brought a problem for my mother, for when she was invited to give guest lectures she would be asked to defend or denounce my critique of the university she happened to be visiting. She found herself caught between maternal pride and the instinct not to offend. I know she had wanted the book to be "nicer", softer in its criticisms. "Surely this university must have some good points," she would say searchingly as I showed her the drafts. "Can't you try and find something nice to say? I'm sure the people who attend this school *believe* it is a very good school. . . . "

Although she joked that she was sorry that I would have to flee Canada after the book's release, she convinced me that she was proud of the result.

In the early nineties, I edited *The Newsmakers*, made a video version of my guide to universities, and wrote freelance articles.

Time spent apart from my mother was painful, for both of us. After a trip to Israel which she had encouraged, I became so attached to the country, I floated the idea of a longer stay; perhaps I might even emigrate. An emotionally and financially excruciating tug-of-war followed on the telephone until I agreed to fly home to talk about it. My mother cried a river of tears until I promised to stay in Canada. It was irrelevant to her that I had met a man there that I believed myself to be in love with. "I need you more," she told me, "and I deserve you more." She persuaded me. It helped that I was beginning to think the man a cad.

This is not to suggest that she wished an isolated spinsterhood on me. On the contrary. Once, when I had confided to her that I was involved with a man who was physically cold, she said bluntly, "Forget about him, Girlie. Marriage without sex is death. Get yourself someone who makes your heart pound." The sooner I found this person, the better. She was fond of saying, "The wedding's all planned, all we need now is a groom." And as the years passed and I remained unmarried, she would add, "Maybe we don't even need a groom. We'll have the wedding and tell whoever it is you end up with about it afterward."

Her impatience to see me wed did sometimes lead to bad advice. When I told her of my plans to ditch a nice but boring man I had dated briefly, she persuaded me to give him "more of a chance", hoping, I suppose, that the prospect of a dull husband would eventually begin to appeal to me. Finally, unable to bear the stupefaction, I told her, over coffee of course, that I had to break off with him.

As she berated me for being too demanding and picky, I told her that such comments were not comforting when my predicament was harder on me than on her.

Leaving the café we passed a bookstore. In the window was a glossy anthology of historical love letters edited by Antonia Fraser. My mother grabbed me by the arm, pulled me inside the store, and handed the clerk her Visa card.

"I'll take a copy of that book in the window," she told him. Turning to me and brushing a piece of hair out of my eyes she said: "I don't want you to think I don't understand about love."

(A year after my mother died I married my boyfriend Tim. The marriage did not last, but it is a consolation to me that, as I planned the wedding without the person who had most wanted to attend, after so many conversations, I knew her wishes *exactly*: I knew the cut of the dress, the number of candles — "hundreds and hundreds and hundreds" — how to arrange the music. The day after the wedding, I took my bridal bouquet — white bleeding hearts and blue forget-me-nots from my mother's garden — and placed it on her grave. It was an inappropriate gesture. My mother had been very much with me the day before.)

One form of love my mother understood particularly well was that between pet and master. "There are days I love dogs more than people," she would admit.

My mother was partial to poodles. The only one of her four dogs who wasn't a poodle was a vicious Lhasa apso, so unpleasant that when she died by gorging herself on mouse poison, we felt guiltily unmoved.

People generally did not understand the pampering my mother lavished on her fourth dog, Diva. But to my mother, Diva was not really a dog but "a girl in fur", with "nothing but kindness in her eyes." She was my mother's constant companion, her therapist, her jester. I'm proud to say that Diva was a surprise birthday gift to my mother from me the fall before she started *The Journal*. My mother wanted a new dog — the others mentioned above had each met untimely deaths by then — but she feared she would lack the time for one, given long *Journal* hours. I had just returned from a vacation in France where I was reminded of the Parisian habit of treating dogs, poodles anyway, as respected citizens. "What about taking the dog to work with you?" I suggested, and she agreed that it sounded like a fine idea. She guessed that Mark Starowicz and the CBC brass would not be keen, but for an acutely perceptive person, she had a convenient way of failing to notice some things. "Mark hates Diva," my mother admitted to me, "especially when she comes into his office with me for meetings and sits on his sofa. But that's too bad." As Vicki Gabereau commented on her show in November 1995: "The only one at the CBC who was ever allowed to bring a dog was Barbara Frum and she could have brought an elephant."

Diva was worth all the ridicule she brought my mother. And there was plenty. Gary Dunford made her a regular topic in his *Toronto Sun* column:

Meet Diva, Barbara Frum's adorable dog. Page Six has whispered how the pretty poodle sometimes sits on the star's lap during hairstylings in network makeup rooms.

Page Six has leaked reports the dog spritzes scenery. So perhaps it was only a matter of time 'til the most terrible tale of all arrived. A night ago, the small black poodle was at the CBC during *The Journal* telecast and dropped — in the words of witnesses — a "substantial" and "decent" doggie-dump on the floor. Employees refused to stoop or scoop Diva's dog doo-doo. Such duties are not in the master contract. But owner Frum and the animal escaped in her husband's Jaguar before the no-way-Jose staffers could press her to do it herself. And three hours after Frum left, the dump was still perfectly in place, exactly where it fell.

If this story is true, and it may be, I can only say in my mother's defence that she cannot have noticed the doo in question. For the number of times she left such a thing unattended, there were many more when Barbara Frum, crouching in a silk Valentino or Montana outfit, conscientiously scraped up Diva's souvenirs.

Because she had difficulty acknowledging that Diva was merely a dog, my mother would be disappointed when her dog insisted on acting like one: eating sandwiches off producers' desks, or, as she once did, rifling through a house-guest's luggage until she found and devoured three boxes of Godiva chocolates. My mother flagrantly ignored the CBC cafeteria staff's written requests that Diva not be brought into their eating sanctuary. ("What? Do they think Diva's dirty?")

Perhaps because it made her seem more human, the trick of Diva's of which my mother was most proud was her ability to eat individually wrapped pieces of Melba toast by peeling away the plastic. Diva would put her head down, a sound of crinkling cellophane would follow, and after thirty seconds, Diva would pull her head up, the toast gone, the plastic on the floor.

The last time I saw this trick was in January 1992. By that time Diva was ten years old, and her skills were in decline. To me, she seemed to be consuming more of the plastic than was healthy.

"It's a cute trick, Mum, but why don't we just take the plastic off for her?"

"Don't be silly," said my mother, never one to underestimate her dog, "Diva knows what she's doing." Diva choked, honked, and wheezed, but she managed to get through about ten packages. When Diva jumped into the limousine that took my mother and her to work, she would depress the window button with her paw, allowing the cool air to blow on her face. At first, it seemed a lucky accident. But when it happened day after day, it became clear that Diva *did* know what she was doing. My mother was amused and vindicated.

My mother was modest about her own celebrity, but after Diva appeared in a pet-lover's magazine, my mother would remark with pride: "Perhaps you recognize her from her recent *Dogs In Canada* profile?"

The connection my mother felt to animals was perhaps best expressed in a story that came to us in one of the letters we received after her death. A Toronto dog-owner wrote that he had found himself in a veterinary clinic the night my mother was there with the poisoned Lhasa apso. His dog had been hit by a car, and was brain dead. He and his wife sat mournfully in the waiting room trying to comprehend the loss of their much-loved animal. My mother, the man wrote, turned to them and said, "Oh, you look like you've something to be sad about. What happened?" Without immediately recognizing her, the man looked "into those deep, concerned eyes," and "told her the story of the loss of our long-time companion. 'Go and say goodbye to him,' she said. 'You loved him.'" They did: something, he wrote, they would not have thought to do otherwise.

My mother understood people, and understood why people love dogs. In the days and weeks after her death, there was no sight sadder than that of Diva, her nose pressed to the glass of the front door, waiting for her mistress to return. She slumped there, for weeks and then months. The image breaks my heart still.

My mother was a tall woman: five foot seven without shoes. Not that she was often without shoes. There were few things she loved more in life than a new pair of Parisian lifts. She owned a small museum's worth. Her taste in shoes, like her taste in clothing, jewellery, and furnishings, was never staid. Years after she delivered that extraordinary graduation address to my high school class, former classmates would remark: "The thing I'll always remember about that speech are those pink polka-dot shoes." I know the pair: Charles Jourdan, *circa* 1981.

In the area of style, my mother and I had an oddly inverted relationship. I found her taste in clothes wild and shocking, and she thought I should have fun and take more risks. As a teenager, she berated me for reading trashy *Glamour* and *Cosmopolitan* magazines, but thought nothing of buying me an outrageously expensive subscription to Italian *Vogue*.

Few things upset her more than when, in my last year of high school, I went through a stage of buttoned-down Brooks Brothers shirts and Scottish kilts from the Sporting Shop. "Conservative political views are one thing, but do you really need to dress like that?"

With few exceptions, her wardrobe was generously available to me whenever I cared to raid it. And she encouraged, even begged me to raid it. I was wary. My experiences in the Barbara Frum school of aesthetics weren't always happy ones.

My first bra was an example. After pointing out to her that the time had come for me to acquire one of these garments, my mother cheerfully offered to take charge. Soon she presented two Mary Quant bras: one, electric red, the other, electric yellow; both decorated with flying purple elephants.

When I wore one of these outrageous items into the locker room I was quickly surrounded by a group of girls. As they approached, I thought hopefully to myself: Maybe they are staring because they are thinking, Wow! If only *my* mother was hip enough to get *me* a bra like that. Or, maybe they want to congratulate me on my non-conformity.

A chorus of nasty laughter broke out. "See! I told you!" said one, and the rest doubled over in malicious glee.

After that incident I demanded money for the plain, white bra I had wanted in the first place.

"Why do you want to have such ordinary things?" said my disappointed mother. "Why do you think those girls have better taste than you?" Fortunately the fashion crusader was also an indulgent parent and she waved me towards her purse.

She and I were used to this. Over the delicate years of a sensitive youth, I took a number of Barbara Frum fashion risks, including the time I went to junior high in Roman sandals (a gift from a recent trip to Italy) when everyone else was wearing Greb boots; and was reduced to tears within ten minutes of the morning bell. It did so happen that whatever item she pushed was the *ne plus ultra* in chic. When she said: "This is what all the young girls in Milan are wearing and those dolts at your junior high wouldn't recognize beauty if it slapped them in the face," it was true. But my mother, brave individualist that she was, had no clue about the laws of the playground, or of how the taunts and jeers of adolescent girls could wound.

In grade seven, when I desperately needed my ears pierced to mimic everyone else, it was to Madame Non-Conformist that I made my appeal.

My mother's ears were not pierced. She instinctively adhered to the Jewish law that forbids cutting or piercing the body for the sake of beauty. "If God wanted you to have holes in your ears, he would have put them there," she said with the logic of a Jewish Mother. She was consistent. Despite the pressures to stay "young-looking" during her *Journal* years, my mother steadfastly rejected suggestions of a facelift. Even if such a procedure had been possible for her (and given the state of her health it was not) she was philosophically opposed to mutilation for vanity. Permission to pierce ears was denied.

My mother never held a grudge, however. When I did pierce my ears, the week before I left for McGill, she began to give me all of my most beautiful earrings. "Thank God your ears are pierced," she would say. "It makes shopping for you so much easier."

While opposed to surgical methods of self-improvement, she did not object to enhancing the body with flamboyant objects. In Mexico she found large sea shells the colour of turquoise and had them turned into ornate rings that covered more than half her finger. From Yemen she brought back thick slave bands which stretched the length of each forearm. One of her prize items was a choker made of horse's teeth. For appearances at the ACTRA Awards she loyally wore only Zandra Rhodes creations. Her friend Rhodes, an English designer famous for ethereal, jewelled, and printed chiffon gowns, was by far my mother's favourite designer. Rhodes and she shared a taste for dazzle, elegance, and mystery.

Although my mother despaired of my dress, over the years I developed an accurate knowledge of her taste. At *The Journal* she would consult my father about the economy, David on world affairs, and me about her wardrobe. This may sound an insulting division of labour, but I believe my job was the most demanding.

The issue of what my mother was wearing was surprisingly relevant to viewers, including people you'd imagine to be beyond such concerns. A classics scholar at Carleton University took the time to write this letter to the *Globe and Mail* soon after *The Journal*'s launch:

> Long ago, when I was at school, we were taught that Marie Antoinette never wore the same dress twice, and that this accurately indicated serious defects in her character... So why is Barbara Frum now doing the same thing on CBC every night?

Such criticism was hard to accept, since my mother, as she often said, would have liked nothing better than to wear a CBC-issued blazer every night. I helped the best I could, not always successfully. One season, when she had run low on blouses, she asked if I would do some shopping for her. I spent an afternoon hopping around Toronto and came back with eight blouses I thought might work. I bought them (checking the return policy first) and walked over to her dressing room on Mutual Street.

She was excited when she saw the thick garment bags: "You angel! You don't know how much I appreciate this!" Then she gave each one a look: "Bad colour. Boring neckline. No. Nope. Uh-Uh. It's pretty but the fabric won't work on camera." I stood before her, eight rejected blouses in my hands.

"Linda," she said, "those were good tries, but it's tough, isn't it? *Nobody* understands how tough it is."

Chatelaine certainly did not understand. For five years my mother appeared on their worst-dressed lists, dubbed Barbara Frump. In turn, my mother was very cutting about *Chatelaine*'s stuffy taste. "Look at their fashion pages and tell me what those women know about fashion!" she would huff. "I guess they'd like to see me in sailor suits!"

She maintained a sense of humour about it until one year

Margaret Laurence appeared on *Chatelaine's* list of fashion criminals. In a telex sent to the private attention of the editor-in-chief, Mildred Istona, my mother defended Laurence, a woman she did not know personally. "Frum's fashion foibles are absolutely fair game, but Margaret Laurence's feelings are not. The journalistic fun obtained was at the expense of someone who has become a public icon because of talent and insight, not wardrobe, and is without the weapons to respond or to rationalize this damage," my mother wrote.

I can imagine my mother's satisfaction when the urbane Mr. Blackwell placed her on his list of the ten best-dressed Canadian women in the late 1980s.

At least her producer, Mark Starowicz, was sympathetic to my mother's burden. In a speech delivered at the dedication of the Barbara Frum Atrium in the new CBC building after her death, (an honour secured for my mother after Starowicz aggressively lobbied the CBC president, Gerard Veilleux), he remembered her clothing travails:

> Barbara was a person of patrician taste, but she also felt
> it was important to support daring, young designers who
> were just getting established. This sometimes led to prob-
> lems. Such as when she would appear on set with a particu-
> larly flamboyant blouse or sweater. And this conversation
> would ensue on the line linking the Main Desk to the con-
> trol room:
>
> The Daily Editor: "She can't wear that, nobody'll be watching
> the guests."
>
> Director in the control room: "Fine, big shot, you tell her."
>
> "No way, you're the director."

"Well, you're the daily editor. I'm not going down there to censor her blouse."

Barbara, who wasn't sensitive about these things at all, finally said one year: "Why don't you all come down, and we'll go through the wardrobe, and you people censor whatever you don't like." So I'll always remember this annual spectacle: Barbara in the dressing room, standing there in her slip, with a cluster of producers, holding up various blouses and sweaters on hangers to her chest, saying: "I think this one's sweet, don't you?" as producers shook their heads, and she sighed, "Geez, you people are conservative."

In his eulogy at her funeral, Robert Fulford remarked: "What is often said of good poets could be said of Barbara: nothing was lost on her. Her curiosity was infinite; incisive questioning of the world was her private habit as well as her public job. I knew Barbara in many moods, but I never knew her to be bored. Life was an unfolding drama to her, and a drama in which she was privileged to play a role. She was a student of that drama till the day she died."

I would add that one of the skills she brought to her studies was an ability to eavesdrop. (Alan Maitland once called it her "knack at overhearing pertinent conversations".) I think of one vacation I took with my parents at a tiny Caribbean Island resort during the winter of 1990.

The chief attraction of the resort — which had room for only thirty guests — was privacy. Guests were assigned to small cabins along the beach front, set well apart from each other. Except for meals served at prescribed times in an elegant, open-air dining room, guests kept largely to themselves. Certainly we did. But that did not prevent my mother and me from taking a keen if distant interest in the people around us. The first year our attention was fixed on a comical English couple. He was a lord or a duke or some such, very elderly and frail. He got around the island on a motorized wheelchair. To reach the hill-top dining room, he had to be lifted by three resort staff. His wife, a garish woman at least twenty years younger, was clearly tired of her drooling, sclerotic husband. He took thirty minutes to dribble the soup down his chin while she blithely feasted on the lavish buffet. Before and after meals she seemed perpetually surrounded by pastries and exotic drinks, reading novels in her designer swimwear ensembles, doing her best to ignore the man who was clearly paying for the vacation. What we could not understand was why, when this man was so sick, indeed dying, had she brought him to a remote island, with no indigenous population, no medical supplies, no doctors, and from which, under shroud of darkness, there was no possibility of exit?

"We are witnessing an Agatha Christie plot," I informed my parents. "She's brought him here to kill him. He'll have a stroke. It will be twenty-four hours before help can arrive, by which time he will be long gone. And she won't be to blame. It's the perfect set-up."

My mother agreed. My father continued reading.

The very next afternoon, the wife of the lord appeared at the entrance to our cabin.

"Excuse me, madame," she said to my mother. "They tell me in the office that your husband is a doctor."

My mother looked intrigued.

"Yes he is," she said. "Why? Has something happened?"

"It's my husband. He's suddenly become very ill. Do you think your husband could come take a look at him?"

"Sure!" said my mother very excitedly. She called for my father. "Murr! Murr!"

My father roused himself. "Yes?"

"Murr," said my mother solemnly, "this woman's husband is ill, she wants to know if you can take a look at him."

"They told me you're a doctor," the woman added.

"I'm a developer," answered my father looking sternly at my mother. "I used to be a dentist, but I'm definitely not a doctor."

"You did do a very nice job on my chin," my mother chirped in, referring to the bandage my father had applied after she had taken a fall on our first night on the island.

"But I'm not a doctor," said my father firmly. "You're going to have to have one flown in."

"Well," said the woman with impatience, "we are preparing to leave the island to go to Grenada. But I thought maybe you could look at him while we were waiting. The boat won't be here for quite a few more hours."

"Sorry," said my father.

When she left, my mother and I tore into him. "But Murr! It would have been so interesting."

"I didn't come on vacation to get sued," replied my father retreating to his chaise longue. "I can just picture it. I touch him. He dies. Then it's my fault. No thanks."

We had to agree that he was right about this. And it was true that he *wasn't* a doctor, even though my mother gave him, among his many roles, that of personal physician. It was his second opinion she sought whenever she needed one.

My mother's infinite capacity to absorb and be interested in the smallest details, could bring humour and understanding to her life, but also pain. I saw this happen each time I accompanied her to the hospital for her blood transfusions during the last year of her life. I would appeal to her not to peer into every room she passed in the hallway on our way to the transfusion rooms, which held four patients at a time. The expression on her face grew darker and darker as she caught images of the very sick and emaciated patients on the "blood" floor. I would say, "Just keep your eyes forward.

Look straight ahead," but I could never sway her. "No," she would respond, continuing to stare at the other patients, "I need to know where I am heading."

During the transfusions themselves, which took four or five hours, it was part of our ritual that I bring a selection of newspapers, magazines, and books, and she would choose from among them what she wanted read to her. I was aware that she paid less attention to the words than to my voice, which comforted her just as hers had comforted me when I was scared and in the hospital.

Whenever a doctor came into the room to talk to one of the other three patients, shielded from us by curtains, my mother would bring a finger to her lips, to hush me. I did not quite approve her habit of eavesdropping in a hospital, where all around us were the terminally ill, many of them young. I knew that if I was oppressed by the problems around us, so was she.

"I'm just at the good part, Mum," I would tell her. "I can't stop here."

An angry look of maternal authority would shut me up, but when the dialogue between doctor and patient became too gruesome, I would try again to distract her.

"Mum," I would whisper, "that patient has AIDS. That's a different problem from your problem. What are you going to learn by listening to that? And anyway, you're being rude. It's none of our business."

Genuine anger would reappear on her face. I shut up and she listened.

When the doctor left the room she would say to me: "What do you think of that? Poor man! That doctor clearly doesn't know *what* to do with him."

And I would say stubbornly, "I wasn't listening. I have no opinion."

I realize now that I should not have begrudged my mother her coping mechanisms. This was yet another thing I learned — a little late. I knew it, though, by the time I received a call from Jay Scott the morning after my mother died. My mother and Jay were good friends, and my mother had been especially solicitous of Jay's lover, Gene, before his death in 1989. When I first picked up Jay's call, I remember thinking how morbid and intrusive his questions about my mother were. Unlike everyone else who called and wanted to know how we were doing and the time of the funeral, Jay wanted to hear *how* she died, her state of mind, the sequence of events, the physicality of it. Although it was painful to supply what he wanted, his unflinching curiosity was now familiar to me. I recognized and knew then what I hadn't known before, that he was also dying. I urged him to join us at the funeral and he told me he would try, but did not appear. I recognized that too. For the last two years of her life, my mother had also been unable to make herself attend funerals, even those of close friends. Jay Scott died fifteen months after my mother.

Epilogue

Seeking for Permission

BARBARA FRUM:

I want to ask about how much a woman can defy age. You so far — touch wood, I hope it goes on forever — defied age. Do you think you can pull it off forever?

SHIRLEY MACLAINE:

Well, I'm already living in forever...

THE JOURNAL, *September 1985*

ON MARCH 11, 1992, my mother conducted her final interview. It was with Mordecai Richler. She felt dizzy, feverish and short of breath. Earlier in the day, colleagues who saw how ill she was — but still did not know the worst — had suggested she skip the interview, and go home to bed. But it was too important to her. "We knew this could be a problem interview," remembers the producer of the piece. "Barbara did not want the program to be seen as promoting his dramatically stated views. It wasn't just the material, it was the tone. She wanted the right tone."

Richler's book, *Oh Canada! Oh Quebec!* was stirring anger and controversy in his home province (several Bloc Quebecois MPs had proposed that it be banned). During the interview, my mother asked Richler if his book might not be harsh and inflammatory. Although she and Richler were both federalists, it is fair to say that my mother was more apologetic towards separatists, and felt a responsibility to help explain their attitudes to English Canadians. She felt that Richler's desire to embarrass the people of Quebec could have the political consequence of trying strained relations between English and French speakers. But Richler felt compelled to write the truth as he saw it:

BARBARA FRUM:

Mordecai, if contemporary expressions of anti-Semitism have disappeared, is it useful to bring up the past and perhaps to over-emphasize it? Like, have you potentially made too much of that one aspect because it troubles you?

MORDECAI RICHLER:

I don't think so. I mean, to some extent, nationalism was rooted in anti-Semitism. I mean, why am I referred to in *La Presse* as "*l'écrivain juif* Mordecai Richler?" I mean, do they refer to Michel Tremblay as "*l'écrivain catholique*" or to Alice Munro as "the Protestant writer?" No, I mean, there...not a word of this. I'm a Quebecker as much as Michel Tremblay. Why am I referred to as l'écrivain juif? Now whoever wrote that would be astonished if I accused them of anti-Semitism.

BARBARA FRUM:

And you don't sit and weigh: Might this be unhelpful at this time? That's not your business?

MORDECAI RICHLER:

Well, I'm trying to tell the truth. I don't think that it's

something that has to be in season, like hockey or hay fever. I think you should be able to tell the truth at any time. And if it makes people uncomfortable, I can't help it.

BARBARA FRUM:

Is it helpful? Is it possible to ridicule people into doing what you want them to do?

MORDECAI RICHLER:

I wasn't ridiculing the people. I was ridiculing the law. And the law is ridiculous. . . .

If my mother had hoped to represent the French Canadian perspective in the interview, she failed. One week later, Lise Bissonnette, publisher of *Le Devoir*, and a woman with whom my mother had a collegial relationship, wrote an editorial about the Richler interview, a portion of which was reprinted in the *Globe and Mail*:

"A more Rhodesian scene than that one would have been difficult to imagine," wrote Bissonnette, comparing my mother to a "high-society matron serving tea in her Salisbury villa to a poor disaffected neighbour, who complains that the servants are ingrates."

By the time Bissonnette's piece appeared, my mother was in the hospital. When my father brought the *Globe* article to her attention, she said to him: "Murray, you must get Lise on the telephone immediately. I must speak to her. She doesn't understand what I was trying to do. She doesn't understand at all. I need her to understand."

My father and I looked at my mother in astonishment. All week he had been presenting her with stacks of telephone messages and my mother had yet to return any of them. She never would. By this point she was so frail, holding a telephone exhausted her. My father tried and failed to reach Bissonnette on my mother's behalf. For several days, with extraordinary effort, she dialed Bissonnette herself. Bissonnette was the only person, outside family, to whom my mother attempted to speak in the last two weeks of her life. My mother left her messages but there was never a conversation. The alienation of Canadians from one another was a final, painful preoccupation. In this respect, she died unquietly.

It had been on the afternoon of the Richler interview, that my father had received a telephone call from my mother explaining that she needed him to pick her up and take her to her doctor. When my father arrived ready, she insisted that he wait until she had taped the: "Good-Evening-I'm-Barbara-Frum" and "Good-Night" segments of the show so that the producers would not be left hanging.

By the time they arrived at the hospital, around five in the afternoon, my mother had a temperature of 103 degrees. The doctor took one look at her and told her that she needed to be admitted.

When my father called me shortly after with this news, I felt less anxiety than I should have. I was living in denial and I took the information calmly.

"It's just a fever," my father told me. "The doctor is checking her now. She'll just be in here a night or two — long enough to run some tests. But nothing to worry about. Now, why don't you get a piece of paper, and I'll give you a list of things you should pick up for Mum from the house. You know, a nightgown, a toothbrush, that book she's reading on the Congo. And then, why don't you pick up some Chinese food and we'll all have dinner together?"

It was this quality of my father's — his confidence, his control, his brightness, the sense of authority — that made everything he said sound reassuring. My mother, and indeed all of us, relied on his strength and good cheer, knowing that whatever crisis arose, we could count on him to make decisions.

"When it's the end for me, I'll know, because I'll see it in Murray's face," my mother confided, but she was wrong. My father's face never betrayed him because he never lost hope. He did not know how. When my mother looked into his eyes, she could only see love and a total conviction that God would protect his wife. Throughout their marriage, my mother had tried to get my father to see the dark underside of life, so visible to her, but had always failed.

My father paid the price for that wilful blindness when she did die. He was shattered.

It is very difficult to explain why none of us saw my mother's death coming, as her "overnight stay" stretched longer and longer. The days brought sometimes better news, but more often worse, about her blood counts and her reactions to drugs. In part my mother's intelligence and morbid wit, fully in force until the moment she died, made it hard for anyone, even the doctors and nurses tending her, to accept that this life-force could be stifled.

The only one who really understood was my mother. Standing in front of the bathroom mirror in her hospital room, her hips pressed against the sink, so that she could lean in and get a good view, she fingered a scab at the corner of her mouth and remarked: "My father had a scab exactly like this, exactly this size, and exactly in this spot when *he* died." She made this observation as coolly as a surgeon. Her tone prevented me from panicking. She might as well have been talking about Meech Lake.

"That scab will heal in no time, Mummy. Don't worry." But she would shake her head, clearly thinking to herself that no one understood and that she couldn't stand to make it any plainer.

"They're throwing the book at me," she said after a consultation with one of the doctors.

"Nonsense. They haven't even begun to reach into their bag of tricks," said my father. But my mother was correct.

Members of the family stayed with my mother in shifts during the two weeks she was in the hospital. During my visits with her, I would massage her feet with cocoa butter, bring her sugar-rich mango and guava juice, sit watching videos with her on the large television set my father had brought from his office. Against my better judgment, I also agreed to smuggle in coffee from the lobby stand. I cringed to think of that black liquid going into her empty but horribly swollen stomach. I knew that coffee (though it can inject a sense of vitality more potent than a bag of hemoglobin) was not going to make her better.

She knew it too.

"I'm dying, Linda," she said to me one day in the hospital as we sat alone together. "I've accepted it and you have to too."

"I don't."

"You have to."

"No Mum, I don't have to. And I won't."

I do not wish to portray my mother as fearless. Her brother Gerald said at her memorial: "In the hospital in the last few days before she died, Barbara refused to believe that she was courageous. She thought that people with courage felt no fear. Barbara was never fearless. She was often afraid and very vulnerable. But even as a child she would not yield to her fears or allow them to govern her actions. Barbara could not be intimidated."

She was not intimidated.

On the afternoon of the day my mother died, she told me in the most direct way what was going to happen later that night.

We were alone again, just the two of us. She was feverish, drained, and depleted. She looked at me beseechingly: "Murr says I have to hang on. Murr says I have to hang on for him. But Linny, I can't." She shook her head vigorously at that and repeated, "I can't."

"But you must, Mummy. You must. So many people need you."

"You don't understand!" she said still shaking her head, angry and pleading. "I can't. I just can't."

My mother's sense of responsibility was so great, she was asking permission to die. She needed permission to leave us. And although I realized it was cruel of me not to give it to her, I could not. We had had this conversation before. Several times in the months preceding her death, as she grew weaker and weaker, she had warned me that if her disease progressed beyond the point where she could maintain her dignity and independence, she would kill herself. I was appalled at this idea and told her so.

"Your life could never be a burden to us," I told her, attempting to address her fears.

"I will never *allow* my life to be a burden to you," she replied firmly.

Shortly after midnight on March 26, my mother died. Minutes earlier, my father had left her side so that they both could get some sleep. It is my conviction that my mother chose the precise moment of her death. She waited until my father was on his way home, and in his absence, released herself from her pledge to hang on. For eighteen years she had persevered. She was exhausted.

When my father called an hour later to tell me that my mother was dead, fifteen years of dread and sorrow stored one layer under my skin, burst. Screams convulsed from me. Tim grabbed me, held me, shook me back to sanity. He told me later, "The sound that came out of you — it was as though someone was reaching inside you, tearing out your soul." That is how it felt.

How does one continue after such a loss? In a *Journal* documentary on fathers, Susan Cheever said that as she cared for her father in his last days, she watched him get gradually more ill, and comforted herself by reasoning: "Well, this is okay. He's just a little sicker than he was before." Each day she told herself the same thing. Finally, when she confronted his dead body lying on the bed, she told herself: "Well, this is okay. He's just a little sicker than he was before."

Human hope is powerful. For the first weeks after my mother died, I would have dreams that the cure for leukemia had been found and was so effective, that it raised even those already dead. Returned from hospital, looking completely well and revived, I would say to my mother with immense relief, "Whew, that was close!"

As time passed, I travelled the stages of grief. My mother continued to appear in my dreams, but she would be disturbingly out of reach, unable to hear me, unable to see me. I would scream to get her attention, but I was invisible to her. In the mornings I would wake with the most terrible pain.

My brother David described his grief this way: "It's like standing on the back of a train, and you watch Mum get off. And then the train pulls away taking you farther and farther away from her."

In December 1993, I had one of those extraordinary life experiences; and though I am not inclined to believe in the supernatural, it turned my head. To explain the event fully I must go back to those walks I would take with my mother, where we would share our most trivial and passionate thoughts. One of her most cherished fantasies, which she spoke of often, was that I would some day make her the grandmother of twins. Each time she expressed this idea to me I would laugh. "Mum, get over it," I would tell her. "I'm not going to have twins! How could I have twins? No one in our family has ever had twins."

"But," she would complain, referring to her friend June Callwood, "June has twin granddaughters! And they're so adorable. You should hear her stories about them. I want twin grandchildren, too!"

"Sorry, Mum, but it's not exactly the kind of thing that is in my control."

A year-and-a-half after my mother's death, in December 1993,

Tim and I showed up at a lab for an ultrasound, eighteen weeks into what had been an unremarkable pregnancy.

To ease my anxiety (we were there after all to find out if there was anything wrong with our child) I chatted compulsively with the technician. At one point he interrupted me to ask: "Were you on fertility drugs before your pregnancy?" I assumed that this was standard technician-talk, and blithely answered, "no," then added, "but it's funny you should ask that because I'm at work right now on a documentary about assisted motherhood," and off I went again.

Finally, when the technician finished the exam, he snapped off his gloves, and in the most casual voice imaginable, said: "You know there are two of them in there, don't you?"

It would be difficult to describe the shock. I asked him to repeat what he meant, told him he was mistaken, told him he was a joker, accused him of playing with my mind and then burst into tears. Thankfully, Tim knew enough to be jubilant. All I could think was: "I have to tell Mum. I need to tell Mummy."

And then it occurred to me. She knew. Of course she knew. She had already told me, long ago, that she would send them. When my children, Samuel Harold and Barbara Louise, were born, I felt the presence of her spirit. And in those two children, I believe, or perhaps, I hope, there is some of the goodness of their extraordinary grandmother.

I'm not quite sure what my mother would have thought about such an idea. Her Jewish identity was emotional not spiritual. Her beliefs — about life after death, heavenly spirits, God — were not well-formed and seldom articulated.

I was with her at an afternoon service for Yom Kippur in 1990. Sundown was approaching, the end of a long day's prayers — although my mother and I had arrived after most of them. To conclude the service, the congregation chants, "May you be inscribed in the Book of Life."

As we said this, a beam of sunlight broke through the window, illuminating my mother's face. It was singular, brilliant, narrow; it shone on her only. It was amazing.

On the walk home, I ventured, "He was talking to you." I was an atheist, as she knew, and looked for her reaction. "I think He was telling you that He wrote your name down."

"It's hard not to think so, isn't it?" she said.

We were two unbelievers who wanted to believe. Pascal said that the desire to believe is the beginning of belief itself, but neither my mother nor I had taken it further.

My mother attended synagogue to hear the Hebrew prayers and music. She understood little Hebrew, but was entranced by the sounds and rhythms; services in English had no meaning. She did not worship God in the synagogue so much as reaffirm a connection to her people. She believed it was possible for Jews to be a people even without our religion, but knew that non-religious Judaism was fading away. It was a legacy spent. My generation would have to renew, or abandon it. My brother has ardently renewed:

"What I am interested in is the faith," he says. "If noodle kugel disappears, it doesn't have any importance to what I care about. But to what she cared about, noodle kugel was important."

It was. To my mother, being Jewish meant what you ate — not kosher food, but kugel and blintzes and borscht and kasha — and the music and the lens through which you saw the world. Judaism was respect for history, the sense and knowledge of suffering, a questioning spirit.

When my mother died we observed *Shiva* (in Hebrew "seven", as in seven days). But the second stage of mourning, *Shloshim* ("thirty days") was cut short by Passover, according to Jewish law.

The day before Passover (5752/1992) the rabbi came to our house to guide the family through the ritual closing of *Shloshim*. We walked out the front door, around the perimeter of the house, then re-entered to complete the chapter or cycle. After Passover, began *Avelut* (the final twelve months of mourning).

Passover itself has become the season of my mother's remembrance, bittersweet with the joy she once brought to this holiday (for despite the efforts Jews make at Chanukah, Passover is really the Jewish Christmas, centred as it is around family and the Seder, a ritual meal). My mother prepared lavishly for the Seder. I think of her on the porch one year, shredding potent horseradish by hand, her nose running and eyes tearing as she drolly declared, "Nothing too good for my kinder!"

Jewish custom makes Passover a parable for life after death. In myth, the Jews' slavery in Egypt is earthly life, and the exodus the soul's journey from it, to the promised, heavenly land. Each Passover we ponder that journey, and its destination.

In the years since the death of my mother, Florence's dignity and strength have guided me. Disraeli wrote, "Those who have known grief seldom seem sad."

My grandmother loved her child but mourns her privately. To the world, to her grandchildren and great-grandchildren, she is courageous, undiminished by age, always attentive to our little troubles, almost always silent about her great loss.

In the summer of 1982, when I was nineteen, my mother wrote to me from a trip to Morocco:

> I miss you very much, but I especially miss Florence this trip. I don't know why. You're so young and all your adventures are just beginning. I think it's losing contact with Florence, even for short breaks, [that] makes me appreciate what a fundamental player she is in my life. ... She's a wonderful mother to me, you must admit. She's not just out there living her own life, being thoughtful or silly or selfish or generous in turns, she's

part of my self. A witness and a confirmation. As though I'm not real and what I think or do or see isn't real unless I can share it all with her. I've been reading some wonderful stories in Graham Greene and John Cheever and in every story there's a hateful mother. But what's curious is — not that they're hateful — but that there's always a mother. Which suggests, I guess, that you — poor thing — will never be rid of me either.

Now that my mother is gone, I have lost my witness. I have lost my confirmation. But she was right: I will never be rid of her. I will never wish to be. My mother lives on in my heart in a love that will never release her.

Photo Credits

Index